NEWCASTLE

Edited by Michelle Warrington

First published in Great Britain in 1999 by
POETRY NOW YOUNG WRITERS
Remus House,
Coltsfoot Drive,
Woodston,
Peterborough, PE2 9JX
Telephone (01733) 890066

HB ISBN 0 75431 454 5
SB ISBN 0 75431 455 3

FOREWORD

This year, the Poetry Now Young Writers'
Kaleidoscope competition proudly presents the best
poetic contributions from over 32,000 up-and-coming
writers nationwide.

Successful in continuing our aim of promoting
writing and creativity in children, each regional
anthology displays the inventive and original writing
talents of 11-18 year old poets. Imaginative,
thoughtful, often humorous, *Kaleidoscope Newcastle*
provides a captivating insight into the issues and
opinions important to today's young generation.

The task of editing inevitably proved challenging, but
was nevertheless enjoyable thanks to the quality of
entries received. The thought, effort and hard work
put into each poem impressed and inspired us all. We
hope you are as pleased as we are with the final result
and that you continue to enjoy *Kaleidoscope
Newcastle* for years to come.

CONTENTS

Jon Rose	70
Eloïse Smith	70
Inés Soria	71
Laura Mowbray	72
Emily Robinson	73
Parminder Kaur	74
Gary Kilday	74
Julie Armstrong	75
Victoria Richley	76
Lucy Frances Dowey	77
Jenna Dargon	78
Claire Redhead	78
Jennifer McAvoy	79
Stephen Warner	79
Julie Smith	80
Ashleigh Graham	80
Karl Olsen	81
Nina Lowery	82
Nicola Grant	83
Joanne Shields	83
Amanda Graham	84
Danielle Stafford	84
Sarah Dowling	85
Craig Tippins	85
Louise Armstrong	86
Alison Langley	86
Jemma Iggleden	87
Shaun Jenkinson	87
Emma Oliver	88
Long Hoang	88
Kathryn Morris & Sarah Nassau	89
Gary Whitelaw	89
Lynsey Hinshelwood	90
Joanne Loughlin	90
James Jobson	91
Jimmy Ng & Christopher McDonald	91
Emma Paxton	91
Gillie Kleiman	92

Sacred Heart Comprehensive School

Victoria Parry	179
Jade Adams	180
Helen Chapman	180
Samantha Gourley	181
Deborah Wilkinson	181
Sharon Baird	182
Rachel Cairns	182
Rabiea Rafi	183
Lisa McCarthy	183
Elizabeth Nolan	184
Laura Jane Aitman	184
Nicola Milburn	185
Kate Kilpatrick	185
Victoria Houghton	186
Claire Smith	186

Seaton Burn Community College

Philip Hodgson	187
Sean Bates	188

Walbottle High School

Laura Hopcroft	189
Kellie Walker	190
Kerry Hickman	191
Jonathan May	192
Natalie Connell	193
Andrew Maddison	194
Chris Dobson	194
Kevin Dodd	195
Andrew Ball	196
Gemma Ions	196
Louise Quin	197
Hayley Harland	198
Lisa Aspinall	198
Robert Fenwick	199
Laura Robertson	200
Amy Smith	200
Laurajane Gray	201

The Poems

MY SISTER

When we were younger we played together,
With dolls and on our bikes.
I followed everything she did; her loves
Were always my likes.
We were together playing from dawn until dark,
Whether it be in a sand-pit, or on slides
In the park.
Both of us would share our laughter and
Our tears.
As we did with our little toys, our clothes
And our fears.
It was as these things subsided, that the pain
Set in.
For the years of teenage rivalry were soon
To begin.
Our happy smiles were shattered and
Our faces grew long,
The bickering began and our hatred became
Strong.
And after some time, we forgot how to smile,
But spite kept our heads busy for a while.
And now I've seen it, I'd like to bring
It to a close,
All of this fighting, just a stupid pose.
Remember my sister, how things used to be,
When we played together, you and me.
That needn't be gone, we can still be friends,
For our sisterly bond need have no ends.

Isabel McArdle (13)
Central Newcastle High School

HOT DAY IN JUNE

June! Tiring and the heavy heat brings drowsiness.
The flower-like colours of sari-clad ladies stroll through
India Gate Park.
Gates and windows were opened wide,
When the music comes in from the tide.
Men with families come in from every side,
The entertainer plays with pride,
On a hot day in June.

Noon, sun blazing from the skies,
There are some notes and many were high,
That day there were many pieces played,
The bandstand made a large shade.
On a hot day in June.

The music was enlightening,
It was then I caught the sighting.
It was the parade,
The sounds it made,
On a hot day in June.

Shalu Rehan (12)
Central Newcastle High School

MISSION POSSIBLE?

Paper bag loaded,
he's a man on a mission
people wait for his coming
with anticipation.

Tacked up in leather
like a future James Dean
not stopped by the weather
on his Harley machine.

Screeches to a halt,
saunters to the door
paper in hand
he pushes it forth.

Into the mouth
of house twenty-six,
he pedals off home
mission accomplished!

Helen Mann (12)
Central Newcastle High School

BABY

A baby runs free,
His fragile body racing like a top horse
Over the fresh wet soil.
His body exposed to the elements
A high pitched giggle is freed from the baby's small mouth
And escapes into the grey clouds above.
He runs towards me, his feet beating the ground.
As he runs near I see his pale skin
As white as the snowdrops beneath his feet
And his pink cheeks as red as the robin's breast in the tree.
The incoming child is running down the hill,
The sun setting behind him
His warm breath in the cool air makes clouds in front of him.
I want him to wrap his freezing arms around my legs
More than anything.
When he does I bend down and kiss his warm head.
His freezing body sends a chill up my spine.
I can smell the sweet smell on him that children capture
In their mother.

Rowann Blair (13)
Central Newcastle High School

THE SMOKER

A crown of smoke
Hangs above him
Poison gas
His lungs breathe out

We shield our faces
Hold our noses
Move off the blue bench
Away from him as

Shrouded in smoke
Clouded he sits
Oblivious to our
Disgust

On and on
The smoke expands
Thick and hard
To peer through.

The train moves in
Brown mingles with grey
Smoke
We jump on

Take deep breaths
Of relief
Though we know
He'll be back
Tomorrow
And everything
Will repeat
Itself again.

Emily Lois Pollard (12)
Central Newcastle High School

PATCH

With a flick of his tail
And a shake of his head,
A stretch and a yawn
And he was up from his bed.

He started to run,
All the way up the drive.
As he saw me go inside,
He started to cry.

He stood there for hours,
Crying at the door.
Gazing longingly up,
At the topmost floor.

I heard him from my room,
And I tried to ignore,
The cries and screams
That made my heartache sore.

As the cries went on,
I could bear it no more.
I ran downstairs
And flung open the door.

Patch jumped in my arms
And started to purr,
And I hoped ignorance like this
Would never again recur.

So that's a tale of my cat,
Yes the one named Patch.
He loves me to bits
And I love him back.

Emily Kent (12)
Central Newcastle High School

AN EQUINE DEDICATION

(This poem is dedicated to two wonderful equines, who have and still are helping me fulfil my burning ambition to be a good horsewoman)

Titchie the little Dartmoor will always be the best,
Not seeing her every day will prove a lifelong test.
She would lighten up a dull day whinnying towards the gate,
Not a second I spent with her could I ever hate.
I dream of riding her once more along a sandy beach,
I doubt there would be anything I would need to teach.
Although she found jumping hard, she'd always try again,
With her small frame, innocent face, and her flowing silky mane.
But now I have Kara, a gentle, beautiful horse,
Who is my dream come true, and will tackle any course.
The impatient excitement pants in her every vein,
Her huge and professional talents are bound to win her fame.
She has a rhythmic gallop, that echoes through the clouds,
And always is attentive with head high, and looking proud.
Shining hooves, pricked ears and legs neat and elongated,
Chasing for her round fields does not fill me with hatred.
Arches her elegant neck, looks with a dark fiery eye,
When looked into, creates mystery and induces a burdened sigh.

Kara and Titchie are both dreams in their individual ways,
Although, to me they're equal, with their warm and friendly neighs.

Aimi Duff (12)
Central Newcastle High School

BEEN THERE, DONE THAT

Imagine your mother,
a child as you are,
and doing the things that you want to.
She really must have known
what it was like, back then,
so that's why she doesn't let us now.

Platforms and short skirts,
heels and heavy make-up.
You ask, but she doesn't let,
It's so frustrating, but remember:
            She did it first.

Laura Wilkinson (13)
Central Newcastle High School

THE STALLION

As the stallion ran through the trees
He suddenly stopped and fell on his knees
And there he saw the finest mare
With lovely golden-browny hair.

He watched and waited for a while
But then came a sound heard for a mile
And in galloped the pretty mare's mate
And the stallion knew he had met his fate.

The stallion looked up on the hill
Where the other stallion stood very still
Then they charged, it was such a sight
Then the stallions began to fight.

They fought until the morning dawned
One had lost, the other won
The one who came from far away
Soon settled down and then did stay.

And then one day, one sunny morn
A tiny little foal was born
He needed to be taught to be king of the wood
And his father was the only one that could.

Becky Gray (12)
Central Newcastle High School

AUTUMN MEANS TO ME

Trees expel golden crisps,
And shrivelled up brown and orange paper,
They discard their former shining emerald glory,
For winter will be here soon.
A shimmering skin,
Gradually creeps over the land,
Leaving glittering gem-filled grass,
Skimmed over by the ice,
For frost is upon us.
Fruit trees explode with ripened jewels,
Plums and apples carpet the land.
Horse chestnut trees drop their brown pearls,
Which are packaged in cream silk,
And protected by green hedgehogs.
The conkers shine like great brown moons,
Glinting as the autumn light catches their brassy bodies.
This is what autumn means to me.

Alex Jordon (13)
Central Newcastle High School

BABY

Pitter-patter, tiny feet
On the smooth black floor do meet.
One step, two steps, then a fall
Nothing to hold onto, nothing at all.

When upset, tears will come
Crying, crying for his mum
When he's happy he will smile
In his own unique style.

He has such an easy life
Untroubled by fears or strife.
There is more in store before
He reaches years four-score.

Sarah Bowles (13)
Central Newcastle High School

My Mother Is A Cleaning Freak

My mother likes to wash and iron,
She gets as vicious as a lion,
If we walk on her clean floors,
Or put mucky fingerprints on her clean doors.
My mother is a cleaning freak!

If you give her cleaning stuff,
She will clean up all the fluff.
In every corner, nook and cranny,
She will even clean your granny.
My mother is a cleaning freak!

She cleans my daddy's shirts and boots,
She'll wash the carpets to the roots.
Mud and dirt she'll clean it all,
She'll dance around and clean the hall.
My mother is a cleaning freak!

My mother likes to cook and clean,
Her favourite polish is Mr Sheen.
She can't be here to bid 'Good day'
Because she cannot stop to play.
My mother is a cleaning freak!

Nicola Robinson (12)
Central Newcastle High School

FAMILIES

Families annoy us so much,
When they get on your nerves (weird aunts included)
When they will not allow you to do what you want,
When they shout and tease you about something so insignificant,
That it almost seems stupid but these are the things
Which we remember.

But families are always there for you,
No matter how much you take your anger out on them,
No matter how much you shout at them,
No matter how much you think you hate them,
You love them really,
And would do anything for them,
Right until you are robbed of them,
By something which happens to us all - death.

Helena Strettle (13)
Central Newcastle High School

YOUR FAMILY

The only thing in the world,
Which you can never lose.
The thing that forgives you after an argument,
The thing that supports you during a crisis,
The thing that will give you joy,
The thing that will give you advice,
The thing that will give you happiness,
The thing that will give you love,
Your family.

Laura Turnbull (13)
Central Newcastle High School

CHRISTMAS

Children dream of their favourite toys,
While Santa makes them for girls and boys.
The angel on the Christmas tree,
Looks down on families full of glee.
The snow is lying on the ground,
Christmas jingles make a sound.
This wonderful time of year for giving,
Just makes our life even more worth living.
The stars shine down from up above,
And fill this day with lots of love.
The baubles and nice tree lights,
Make us enjoy these fun filled nights.
It all started on that day,
When Jesus was born upon the hay.
Yes, you have guessed it, you are right,
This time of year is Christmas night.

Kate Crosby (12)
Central Newcastle High School

GROWING UP

From crying 'Da Da' then to talking,
From sitting, crawling then to walking.
You seem to grow up ever so fast,
Your childhood never seems to last.
Your hands may have tripled in size,
You have grown knowledgeable and wise.
With your parents you have a special bond,
The memories of childhood I recall are fond.

Lucy Healer (13)
Central Newcastle High School

A POD OF WHALES

Sleek and graceful;
Frighteningly powerful,
Rulers of the sea.
With clicks and squeaks,
Many voices -
Pass through the pod.

Gentle and intelligent,
Maternally proud,
Comes new life.
With suckling and affection,
Growing strong -
But always keeping close.

Restless and wondering,
Always moving,
Following ancient trails.
With fins and tails,
Breaking surface,
In playful moods.

Young and old,
Many relations -
Swim as one.
With many generations,
Survived disasters -
They're here to stay.

Zoë Bellamy (13)
Central Newcastle High School

ONE APPLE

The leaves start browning,
Like a cake, that's been left in the oven too long.
The trees start swaying,
Like an old lady's skirt.
Still, only one apple left on the tree.

The leaves gently fall,
Like a parachute gliding through the air.
The wind starts to whistle,
Like a balloon, slowly losing its air.
Still, only one apple left on the tree.

The leaves start to dry out,
Like some clothes on a washing line.
The wind grows colder,
Like a person, very bitter.
Still, only one apple left on the tree.

The leaves blow along the street,
Like lettuce, being tossed in the salad.
The wind starts to whoosh,
Like a whip smacking the floor.
Still, only one apple left on the tree.

The leaves are few, left on the crooked hand,
Like a woman with only three hairs on her head.
The tree is now bare,
Like a baby, only just born.
The one apple left, falls to the ground.

Sarah J G Jamieson (13)
Central Newcastle High School

GRANDMA AND ME

Grandma
The smell of home-made bread,
Rising on the range each day.
Washing through the mangle,
Out in the back yard to play.
Getting up early to walk to school,
Two miles each way.
Hot water for the tin bath,
But only on Sunday!
Coal down the coal chute,
For the roaring fire on a winter's day.
At harvest time helping,
To gather in the hay.

Me
Heating at the flick of a switch,
No need for a fire all day.
Clothes washed and tumble-dried,
And neatly put away.
Run a bath any time I want,
Computer games to play.
A TV in my bedroom,
Lots of friends to stay.
Go to school by car or train,
No need to walk each way.
Ready cooked meals in the microwave,
Which child lived the better way?

Lucy Milner (13)
Central Newcastle High School

Advice To An Older Brother Now You're Thirteen

I used to think
you were God,
whenever you spoke
I felt honoured.

You are my big brother,
you were my friend
but now you've changed
now you're thirteen . . .

We've made videos,
heard tapes, seen pictures
but your head is all that counts
when it comes to memories.

Whenever I needed advice
your mouth would open
and you would come running
but now, now you're thirteen . . .

Don't forget me,
shirts rip, cars break
and girls leave
but I'm here for life.

You would take me
to the park or cinema
but not now
now you're thirteen . . .

I'm not an item,
I'm your sister.
I love you
Never forget it.

Faye Coats (12)
Central Newcastle High School

HERE I LIE

My peaceful island, my beautiful sea,
The world I live in, my tranquillity.
The days and nights I've spent alone,
My comfort is the sea's soft moan.

The creatures that share in my world,
Know that I watch, as their lives are unfurled.
And the plants that bloom beneath the sun,
Understand that I - with them - are one.

My faithful companion, the one I love most,
Not a being or one seen only by ghosts.
Is the sea, whose soft whisper is with me always,
In my thoughts and my feelings and all of my days.

But now the waves have lost control,
My island is no longer whole,
The sea is tearing it apart
And soon it will tear up my heart.

The waves come crashing down on me,
My soul is thrown up by the sea,
My beauty and my grace are gone
As the waves sing their wrathful song.

The anger the sea shows, it fills me with alarm,
I try to hide from it, to keep me from harm,
But the storm it still catches me, though I am not wet,
Just the death of my island makes my future all set.

'It's all too perfect,' some did say,
And I agreed in every way.
But now I look back as my heart is broken,
And see that truer words have never been spoken.

Here I lie, on the seabed
And here I'll stay, to rest my head.

Rachel Steele (12)
Central Newcastle High School

MY GREAT GRANDMOTHER

My great grandmother
I used to see,
She would never stop
Nagging me.

Even though I saw her
About once a week,
She would always grab a hold
And nip my cheek.

But on these visits
We would sit,
Listening to the time
She nearly worked down a pit.

For hours she'd talk,
She could yatter all day
But thankfully that wasn't
The length of our stay.

I wouldn't have minded
Except for one thing
Her stories like a bell
Always ding a ding, ding.

Lucy Cullen (14)
Central Newcastle High School

HE GROWS SO FAST

First day home from hospital,
No longer alone,
Responsible for another life,
Totally in control.

Baby grows so fast,
From toddler straight to teenager,
In no time at all,
It all feels so fast.

Soon he is grown up,
With a family of his own.
That first day mother,
Is now a first day grandmother.

Alison Cubbins (13)
Central Newcastle High School

SISTERS

The bond between sisters is said to be strong,
But I know that breaking it won't take long.
One nasty word, one simple lie
Then the bond will crumble and then soon die.

But the hatred that follows is doomed not to last,
And all is forgotten and put in the past.
'But why is this so?' I hear you all say,
I know not the answer, it's always this way.

Are ties this weak, that break at a blink,
Not worth having? And this makes me think,
The bond between sisters is perhaps not that strong,
But deep down inside I know I am wrong.

Abbie Waller (13)
Central Newcastle High School

MY DARLING LITTLE SISTER

My darling little sister
Will chatter all day long,
Her tongue just keeps on wagging
Like a puppy dog's tail.

My darling little sister
Follows me round the house,
She trots behind me all the time
Just like that little dog!

My darling little sister
Tries to join in with my friends,
She draws all over my posters;
I'd rather own the dog!

Nathalie Boobis (14)
Central Newcastle High School

AUTUMN

Autumn shows her chilling presence,
Swept in on a gust of leaves,
Coloured swirlings, whirlings, twirlings,
In rusty brown, scarlet-red and greens.

Winter is heralded by autumn,
In autumn the skies are grey,
The roads are coated in ice.
The cars now slip and sway.

I love the start of autumn,
Romance is in the air,
Christmas is drawing near,
People start to prepare.

Sarah M Brown (12)
Central Newcastle High School

ELSIE

A lifeless lump of wrinkles and wiry hair
Silently wears away the rockers on the old, wooden chair.

A piece of furniture,
  She still collects dust,
    Needs to be hoovered around,
      And requires the occasional polish when friends come to stay.

An agony aunt,
  She has the advice for every imaginable scenario,
    Never failing to please,
      If only you would ask.

A living library,
  She contains decades of information,
    If only you will delve in to find it.

A low maintenance hoard of information,
  A personal advisor,
    A friend.

So why is this fountain of knowledge silently wearing away
The rockers on the old, wooden chair?

Holly Donowho (13)
Central Newcastle High School

THE ALIENS

Quietly they descend on their lighted spaceship,
Into the large field they walk, exploring,
Their fluorescent arms glow in the darkness of the night,
While they wonder about the strange things they see.

We watch from our houses quite close by,
While these spectacular creatures search our planet.
Their circular heads with countless eyes,
Search and search, for what we don't know.

They talk in their language,
It sounds like gobbledegook to me.
We silently watch while the creatures approach,
Never knowing their next move.

Questions race through our minds,
Like a runner going for gold.
Why are they here?
What are they going to do?

Roona Bhatt (12)
Central Newcastle High School

FLYING

I wish I could fly!
If I could . . .
I would glide swiftly
Over the treetops,
Making the trees ruffle
Like a cold pigeon.
I would swoop down low,
And sip from the moon's lake.
I would soar up high,
As high as a bald eagle,
Then come crashing down
Like lightning in a storm,
Making time stop.
I would flutter above calm waters
Leaving flawless ripples behind.

Zakia Arfeen (12)
Central Newcastle High School

THE SHADOW

The boat crashed through the fierce waves
As the shadow glided from its cave,
The motionless fish lay on the deck,
The fish the shadow craves.

The shadow was too far left
And took a turn for the right,
And from the fish's corpse
The shadow took a bite.
It was clear to the sailor
That the shadow was a shark
A thirteen foot long Great White.

The sailor drew his harpoon gun,
And shot the harpoon, the deed was done,
The sailor jumped for joy,
As the terrible sport to him was fun.

The sailor headed for the shore,
The corpse dragging along,
As the sailor went on his way
He sang his sea shanty song.
When he arrived at the shore
A huge crowd had gathered,
But they didn't cheer or praise the sailor
To them the deed was wrong.

Sarah Barrass (12)
Central Newcastle High School

The Old Oak Chair

There stands the old oak,
Where three generations have passed.

Once sat there in the old oak chair,
My grandfather smoking a pipe,
Twenty years old,
When the winters were cold
With no heating to keep alight.

Twenty years later
When there were more to cater for,
There sat my mother
In that same oak chair,
With no cares in the world,
Choosing one from the other
The chair still stood there,
Almost forty years old.

Now sit I,
Not too young to appreciate,
The importance of this dear oak.
I dedicate the family to carry
On the charity of the memories
To other folk.

Anoushka Jahangiri (14)
Central Newcastle High School

THE VISIT

The flesh had perished off the face,
I looked again there was no trace.
That evil face, that haggard grin
I thought again should I go in?
What had she done before in time
To make me fear this life of mine?
I realised I must obey,
All I could do was stand and pray.
'Come in' I heard the awful voice,
My hands and neck were very moist.
I look up, I did see,
Those hideous eyes boring down through me.
The room that I was standing in,
Was small and brown and very dim.
Then she slammed the heavy door,
My pounding heart could take no more.
I opened the door and oh how I ran,
I didn't know it was such a torment
To see old Gran.

Laura Steen (13)
Central Newcastle High School

THE AFFECTIONATE FELLOW

In the alley at the dark of night,
Nothing to be seen but amber lights,
The bird-watching bandit
Creeps out of the shadow.

A silhouetted black figure
On marshmallow paws,
Affectionate fellow
Leaps up on a wall.

The master of whining
And dining on mouse,
The king of the alley
And the Duke of the house.

On needlepoint claws,
The affectionate fellow,
With sandpaper tongue
Crouches down in the moonlight
And purrs . . . and purrs . . . and purrs . . .

Nicolina Spatuzzi (13)
Central Newcastle High School

PEACE AND QUIET

Nowhere I go can I do my work,
Little bro keeps going on about Captain Kirk.
Mum's reciting her new-found recipe,
Dad's talking to his business pal 'Is it really a necessity?'
Janie's raving about her new skirt from Tammy Girl,
Uncle John just encourages her 'Give us a twirl.'
I go into the garden to find some quiet,
But next door police are trying to stop a football riot.
In the shed birds keep chirping,
And the boy from next door comes to annoy me
With his drink, gargling and slurping.
I hike up to the attic but Matt starts playing his electric guitar,
He thinks that some day that racquet's gonna make him a rockstar.
At last I take refuge in a dark, lonely cupboard,
Then I hear a voice behind me
'I can't find anywhere to do my work
And my teacher's gonna kill me' he blubbers.

Róisín Kelliher (12)
Central Newcastle High School

IN HOSPITAL

I'm sitting in ward number four,
With nurses running through the door.
You'd think they'd keep it fairly quiet,
But near my bed it's quite a riot.

In the room just next to me,
A pile of plaster is all you can see.
I was told there is a man inside,
I suppose he's scared and wants to hide.

A nurse is holding a syringe,
Making everybody cringe.
The poor boy looks like he's got the flu,
The syringe going in . . . 'Ooh.'

It's nearly dinner; the grub's OK,
They bring it on a fancy tray.
I hope the food is good tonight,
Because last week it was a sight.

Before everybody goes to sleep,
The doctor comes in and takes a peep,
At every wound and all our cuts,
He takes our temperature and he tuts.

So that's what life is like in ward number four,
With nurses *still* running through the door.
I'll put my fingers in my ears,
To block out the noise of babies' tears.

Gemma Fay (12)
Central Newcastle High School

MEETING AUNTIE - A SEVEN YEAR OLD'S VIEW

I sit in my (very uncomfortable) seat, quietly awaiting
                                    my imminent doom.
Of course I tried to get out of coming here -
Measles, chickenpox, Arabian whooping cough -
I tried them all, my mum believed none of them.
I slide further down my chair.
Maybe if I make myself look small enough I'll just disappear,
Maybe I could just slip under the table,
Maybe I could hide in the loos,
Maybe . . . no I can't escape.
I stare at the clock; any minute now . . .
Slam! The door is flung open.
A small but powerful vision in a titanic purple feathered hat
Is standing in the doorway.
Slowly, slowly it approaches me,
It is made up very badly in tarty hot pink lipstick
And blue lagoon eyeshadow.
I avoid eye contact, surely it must have been four months . . .
No, it's coming closer, I don't have much time.
Frantically I look for a fire escape, but there are none
There is no escape now.
As the apparition bears down on me I close my eyes,
Help me God!
Then suddenly it's all over, my heart is still pounding.
I look up at my aunt,
I look down, she hands me a tissue.
'Here darling, you've got lipstick all over your cheek'
I shudder, she doesn't realise how scary
                                    getting a kiss off her is.

Esther Sharp (14)
Central Newcastle High School

WINTER, WHICH IS COLD AND HARSH
TO
SPRING, WHICH IS PLEASANT AND SCENTED

Yesterday there was a snowy blanket
Covering the winter's gardens.
Yesterday there were rain crystals
Covering the winter's flowers.

Today there is no blanket
Covering the fresh grass.
Today there are no crystals
Covering the new spring flowers.

Yesterday there were no children
In the streets, playgrounds and parks.
Yesterday there were no birds
In the streets, playgrounds and parks.

Today there are children playing
In the streets, playgrounds and parks.
Today there are birds singing
In the streets, playgrounds and parks.

Yesterday the world was
Cold and harsh.
Today the world is
Pleasant and scented.

Goodbye winter
And
Hello spring.

Kulwinder Gill (12)
Central Newcastle High School

MY KALEIDOSCOPE

Evening sunset and bloodstained red,
Both were going through my head.
Sea, emerald and grass
All float past my eyes,
Yet they're pieces of glass.

There is marigold and sunflower,
Yellows as you know;

Sky, deep sea blue azure and sapphire
Glitter and dance in the sun.

So these are the colours
Of my kaleidoscope,
And they will never leave me
I hope.

Laura Seymour (13)
Dame Allan's Girls' School

KALEIDOSCOPE

Peering deeper, deeper down
Through my kaleidoscope,
A tunnel of many vibrant colours
Unstable and fluctuating,
Life faraway, make-believe lands.
One finger's turn is like a change of worlds,
Like representations of an unpredictable future,
Like outer space, an uneven horizon
Of jumbled moons, stars and shapes,
Waiting for me to encounter!

Jade Sanders (13)
Dame Allan's Girls' School

KALEIDOSCOPE

Born from an orb of burning light, it embraces the flaming horizon
with its reflections.
Eyes dripping with idyllic colour, a thousand shafts of glowing glass
falling into infinite uncertainty.
Clothed in random fluctuations of ever-turning symmetry and housed
in pure, vivid simplicity.
Hands that instigate its boundless changes, within a single cycle of its
walls, cannot govern its consequence.
Creator of a dazzling array of confined intensity, now swimming in
the eye of your mind.
Experiences so vivid, images too heavenly to touch, too real to see
hide behind its mirrored symmetry.
Colours of the world held within an eye, held up to the light,
lucidity ten times greater than before.
Dancing drifts of triangular blue, partner infatuated resplendent red,
whilst resounding to the music of the spheres.
Revolutions of its simple design, let fall the colours into a complex
array of symmetry.
Reality thought to be embracing the eye, a mere illusion hidden by
a mirror, an imitation of beauty.

Frances Smith (14)
Dame Allan's Girls' School

KALEIDOSCOPE

Life, mysterious life.
Ever changing,
Ever moving,
This is the pattern of life.

Life, complicated life.
Intensely real,
Jumbled and complex,
This is the pattern of life.

Life, changeable life.
Random, unstable,
Motley and mobile,
This is the pattern of life.

Life, variable life,
Fluctuating, fluid,
Confused, convoluted,
This, the kaleidoscope of life.

Louise Richardson (13)
Dame Allan's Girls' School

KALEIDOSCOPE

Ruby reds and bronzing browns,
Are they really there?
Lemons, yellows and emerald greens -
Oh why can't we touch?

Sapphire blues and ebony blacks,
Pretty patterns here and now;
All the colours of the world
In this tiny tube.

All around the world goes on
But in this tiny dream world,
Little misshapes of sequinned cardboard
Take you away from reality.

Different colours whizzing round,
It's all really there with mirrors.
All the colours of the world,
In this tiny tube.

Danielle Wood (12)
Dame Allan's Girls' School

KALEIDOSCOPE

My life is like a kaleidoscope,
An ever changing scene;
All the beautiful colours,
Reds and blues and greens.

Completely unpredictable,
A wonderful sight to see;
Sparkling in the sunlight,
It's a mystery to me.

With the violets and the lemons
And breathtaking emerald greens,
How anyone can be sad
Once this magic sight they've seen?

Gemma Thompson (13)
Dame Allan's Girls' School

KALEIDOSCOPE

Patterns shapes, colours too,
Pink, red, green and blue;
Different shapes, patterns galore,
Turn the end to see what's in store.

Changes, reflections, mirrors and images,
The choice you can see it just never finishes.
Colours here, colours there,
Inside are colours everywhere.

In a kaleidoscope there can be found,
Reflected light but never a sound,
A child's toy on a rainy day,
A wondrous thing in every way.

Megan Kelbrick (11)
Dame Allan's Girls' School

THE KALEIDOSCOPE

They shine and glow from down below,
But so close it's like peering through a magnifying glass.
There are many colours from fiery red to sky blue,
Reflected in mirrors many shapes and patterns just for you.

There is no one there, you're on your own,
In a fantasy world of colours and small delicate rainbows.
The patterns are symmetrical, never the same, ever changing.
But so close! Put out your hand and touch the mutable shapes:
They are not there. It's an illusion created by reflection.

All is created by the simple, sleek turn of the notch,
Which makes our eyes see the masterpiece.
It's a mobile, colourful, enchanting kaleidoscope,
An amazing device that produces these dreams.

Nicola Holmes (13)
Dame Allan's Girls' School

KALEIDOSCOPE!

K aleidoscope, so random.
A n illusion, it's not really there.
L ots of shapes.
E ver changing.
I nfinitely variable, so immediate.
D on't try to change it, you can't.
O range, red, blue, they are all there.
S o symmetrical, so intensely real.
C reated by trickery.
O rientated, only to itself, but not to me.
P leased with itself, because it fooled me.
E ventually I have to give it up, it's too hard.

Kirsty Maule (13)
Dame Allan's Girls' School

KALEIDOSCOPE

The swirling sequins,
float silently into the void of space,
ever changing the symmetrical pattern.

Colourful shapes fall more randomly now,
with squares and triangles,
promising a new design every time.

It's an ever changing illusion,
of different shapes and hue
which are all brightly coloured,
green, orange, purple and blue.

The last green sequin is slowly floating down,
down to the bottom of the universe,
settling down for the next victim,
of this fluctuating game.

Sarah Ellam (13)
Dame Allan's Girls' School

KALEIDOSCOPE

A kaleidoscope to me it seems,
Is a world of magic, colours and dreams;
Ever glowing, ever changing,
Pretty patterns rearranging,
Like snowflakes floating in a sunlit sky,
As coloured insects flutter by,
Shining sunbeams bunched together,
It seems to me to go on forever,
As the colours shift like night and day,
The magic slowly fades away.

Harriet Coleman (11)
Dame Allan's Girls' School

KALEIDOSCOPE

A vision of shapes like circles or squares,
Full of unusual colours,
With beauty that might not be seen again,
In a few pebbles and mirrors.

Ebony comes to edge the vision,
But indigo comes in star-like prisms,
Scarlet, crimson, lilac and green,
All of these are often seen.

Exquisite beauty and light at the end,
Makes the image finished and then,
All this beauty can be found,
When rotated round and round.

Louise Needham (12)
Dame Allan's Girls' School

KALEIDOSCOPE

Rotate,
Towards the dazzling light.
Mirrors creating fluid,
Unstable symmetry.
Complex cut glass.
Scarlet, olive, sapphire, gold.

Rotate,
Pointing at the motley sky.
Violet, silver, jade.
Translucent polygons.
Optical shapes created by trickery
Intensely virtual spiralling pieces.

Emma Parker (13)
Dame Allan's Girls' School

KALEIDOSCOPE

Looking through a kaleidoscope
At patterns striped and swirled,
They're patterns ever changing
Your imaginary world.

What you see isn't real,
It isn't really there.
It is just an illusion,
So handle it with car.

The colours may entrance you -
Lapis, gold and jade,
Silver, rose and sometimes bronze
Form the patterns that are made.

The fragments form the snowflake,
Circles, diamonds, squares.
It makes you get the feeling
You're seeing something rare.

Do not be a fool;
See through the mirrored tricks.
The bright colours are random:
The patterns can't be picked.

Looking through a kaleidoscope
At patterns striped and swirled,
They're patterns ever changing;
Your imaginary world.

Polly Procter (12)
Dame Allan's Girls' School

THE KALEIDOSCOPE

The snowflakes fall like an illusion into an infinite life,
The flames engulf them into a world of pain and strife,
The angels who savour their elegant beauty, exist no more,
Nothing the turn of God's hand could restore.

The sunsets of life have risen again,
Those fluctuating colours engaging never to be the same.
Those mutable oranges and complex maroons,
Have gone with the wind into convoluted blues.

Those blues so like water have turned into sea,
Those motile waves spread out like flowers of green.
But the mortality of life will not be ignored,
So the variety of green seems a lot more broad.

The complicated structure of the ice cold night,
Is shown through these purples so heavenly bright.
These symmetrical purples have now changed to dark,
The heaven of colours has extinguished its spark.

As God turns his magic all will seem so clear,
That our lives will be left for us each to steer.
But all lives are special and never the same,
A turn of your hand and your life will feel pain.

But as God turns his hand there is no need to fear,
But in life there is room for more than one tear.
All like a kaleidoscope,
An illusion to Thee.

Kate Hall (13)
Dame Allan's Girls' School

COLOURS OF THE KALEIDOSCOPE

Put your kaleidoscope at ease
Shine it at the sun and look inside
Flashing colours all at once
Turn and twist as you respond.

From deep subtle reds to solitary black
Like those of flames all combined
And vibrant
Pound and leap in my sight.

Circles and shapes let themselves
Float around
Into whirlpools of dimensions
Bouncing into magnificent shapes
Guiding us through tunnels of
Distorted light
In a fever of eagerness.

Yellow fireballs spin and burst,
Green leaves widen and reach out
Orange rinds of burning iron
Overpower us with their
Spiralling chords of magic
Oceans of golden light pour
Into the sparkling kaleidoscope.

The simple cylinder
Deceives you into patterns
Of exploring colour
Caressing you and gradually
Enchanting you
Out of consciousness.

Shapes of wonder let us see,
These symmetrical magical
Images
Infinitely changing shapes
Take over
And steal your breath
Again and again and
Again . . .

Sofia Hassen (11)
Dame Allan's Girls' School

THE KALEIDOSCOPE

Colours of turquoise, fiery red and green,
Shapes you've never seen
Make my kaleidoscope,
Seem like a dream.

With a twist and a turn,
Now I see, a sky full of formation
Just for me.

A meadow full of flowers,
A patchwork quilt,
A jigsaw puzzle,
Of patterns so bright.

A simple tube of trickery, illusion and light
That's a kaleidoscope,
Simple and right.

Victoria Bosi (13)
Dame Allan's Girls' School

KALEIDOSCOPE

Coruscating auroras
Like a daylight sheen
An embodied awareness
Consciousness in a fool's paradise
A sensational feeling,
You're isolated, in a trance
The colours feel imminent
But to touch are so distant
The pattern is infinitely variable
Never knowing where to turn next
Like life
We are able to make adjustments
But cannot compose the result.

Natalie Candish (13)
Dame Allan's Girls' School

KALEIDOSCOPE

Patterns swirling round and round,
Colours moving - they make no sound.

Illusions, tricks, hues and tints,
Violet, berry, jade and mint.

Intangible, unreal, a picture in your mind.
The shapes and complexions, there isn't an end to find.

Forms and shapes with every tone,
Circles, oblongs, spirals and cones.

Kaleidoscopes, like people, different with each turn,
Crimson, azure, copper and fern.

Charlotte Soulsby (12)
Dame Allan's Girls' School

THE MAGICAL HUE IN A KALEIDOSCOPIC VIEW

As I look through this black desolate tube, I see swirls and splats
and things like that.
I see flakes of burnished gold blended in with bits of tangerine orange.
I see sapphire blue with olive green so glowingly bright.
I see violet as pretty as the spring blooms entangled with a
blushing, shy red.
I see an unblemished cyan, injected with a dazzling lemon yellow.
I see a budding green with a rosy pink.
I see ebony black combined with pearly white.
I see Persian blue as dark as black with a tinge of cobalt blue.
I see a cherry scarlet co-ordinated with a chestnut brown.
I see an array of infinite symmetry so fascinatingly bright.
I see shapes of all sizes so eye-catching and enchanting.
That's the kaleidoscopic view for you.

Sneha Prasad (12)
Dame Allan's Girls' School

KALEIDOSCOPE

K aleidoscope.
A uthentically covered
L ike a swift dream.
E very colour in the rainbow,
I ndividual patterns, never the same.
D istinctively designed,
O ver and over again.
S hapes of fragments like a flower,
C lattering down like a shower.
O ptical tricks that never exist,
P atterns symmetrical.
E nding with a kaleidoscopic illusion.

Davina Dhindsa (12)
Dame Allan's Girls' School

KALEIDOSCOPE

Colours as bright as a stained-glass window,
Shining down, highlighting the dozing grannies
The pages sparkling whilst split into hundred of
different shapes and colours.
Many different shades: cyan, cobalt, and yellow
glowing on the page.

The rainbow spreads across the sky representing many things:
God's promise to mankind that there would be no more floods and,
Noah when he first saw the rainbow knew that the flood had ended.

The crisp, golden autumn leaves shining as they fall
silently to the ground;
The reds, yellows, greens, blacks an browns
are good camouflage for hedgehogs,
But soon they just get swept up and put in a bin bag.
No more kaleidoscopic visions left.

Anne Savage (12)
Dame Allan's Girls' School

KALEIDOSCOPE

Timeless trickery in a tin can,
Endless colours spilling like Smarties from a tube,
Small gemstones in a rock pool, opals, rubies, green emeralds too.
A volcano of colour.

Sounds like rain on a corrugated roof,
Like the rattle of hundreds and thousands in a plastic drum,
The sound of a Catherine wheel spinning round and round,
The sound of dead pine needles dropping to the floor.

Timeless trickery in a tin can.

Sophie Egan (12)
Dame Allan's Girls' School

KALEIDOSCOPE

It changes as you turn it.
The patterns are not really there
Just turn it if you hate it
And it's round, not square.

Round and round it spins,
It's all that we see.
Seeing what we want
In an artificial illusion of a world.

The world we live in is stranger than some,
Not hot, red and dusty or colder than ice.
We often complain.
And say that it's not nice;
We changed it to this
Now we have to pay the price.

It's a vicious circle
That no one can break,
We don't ever give - but take.

Pretend we know it all,
Pretend we're in control.
It's just another illusion,
From which we can't escape.

The truth isn't kind,
Who told you that it was?
Ask why we're here
And the answer is because.

It's another unsolved riddle
Like the thoughts inside my head.
Like the kaleidoscope I am.

Rachel Lee (12)
Dame Allan's Girls' School

KALEIDOSCOPE

What do I see
In front of me?
Is it something rare
Or has illusion taken hold?
Is it really there?
It has to be a trick, I see;
Those snowflake patterns cannot be:
Such pretty shapes that are so rare,
I want to touch them -
It's not fair!
But will I ever see
The same pattern in front of me?
Or is that tube I'm looking through,
Changing the patterns, always new?
Is there a secret nobody knows
As the pattern turns and grows?
Patterns and shapes and colours too,
Eternally changing shades of blue,
And other colours, red, yellow and green -
The most beautiful patterns I've ever seen.

Phillida Strachan (11)
Dame Allan's Girls' School

KALEIDOSCOPE

The wheel turns
The colours move
The pattern changes.

The colours - bright
The patterns - beautiful
A mercurial scene.

So beautiful yet
Unpredictable
Uncontrollable.

In awe
We stare down through the tube
But what is it we're seeing?
No more than a few bright colours
Reflected in a few simple mirrors.

Sarah Cameron (12)
Dame Allan's Girls' School

KALEIDOSCOPE

It works as if by magic
And no one knows the trick,
But the illusion is caused by mirrors
And not a magician's stick.

It is not meant for adults
It really is a toy,
But you try telling my mother,
It's only for her girl and boy!

The shapes, they are so pretty
And the colours are so bright,
The patterns are so interesting
They light up in the night.

The patterns go round and round
But as they appear
Without making a sound
They bring music to my ears.

Chloe Luper (12)
Dame Allan's Girls' School

KALEIDOSCOPE

I woke up one morning, surprised to see
A cylinder parcel addressed to me.
I opened it slowly with wide open eyes,
Filled with curiosity to see what's inside.

A kaleidoscope! Is this a joke?
Surely this is a toy for little folk.
Good heavens - I was amazed to see
A magical world was in store for me!

Never the same, forever changing,
Random patterns thrown at you;
Chrysanthemums, snowflakes, a diamond or two,
But all of them random, unseen shapes to you.

Azure, terracotta, cobalt and gold,
And damson and ochre and violet and mauve.
An explosion of colours, a sparkle, a shine,
Illuminating, irradiating is what you will find!

If only I could control the wonderful outcome,
And twist it, and twirl it, to be how I want;
But then it wouldn't be such a surprise,
And the patterns would be so plain to the eye.

It's a secret only I can see, a place that I can visit,
The earth, the moon, the sky, the sun, for colours there is no limit!
But all this is an illusion, an optical trick;
It's not really there, it doesn't exist!

Jo-Anne McClafferty (12)
Dame Allan's Girls' School

KALEIDOSCOPE

Twisting, turning,
Whirling, swirling.

In and out through each other shapes weave,
Forming patterns made to deceive.

Emerald and violet,
Sapphire and scarlet:

Symmetrical patterns made by light.
A different shape comes into sight.

Reflections, illusions,
Deceptions, confusions.

Then gone.
Never again,
Never the same,
Gone!

Katie Siddle (12)
Dame Allan's Girls' School

KALEIDOSCOPE

Patterns, reflections, colours and movement;
Symmetrical shapes, mirrors and illusions;
Forever changing, not the truth, never the same,
Only visible once;
Jazzy movement, whirls and tricks;
Light;
Blurred;
Isn't really there;
Kaleidoscope.

Kirsty Bell (11)
Dame Allan's Girls' School

THE KALEIDOSCOPE OF SARAH'S

When Sarah was a kid,
She always had a kaleidoscope with her.
One day Mummy asked her 'What's so special about it?'
And Sarah answered, 'It's beautiful, it's like a beautiful city!'

Every night she dreamt about her kaleidoscope,
She dreamt she was in the kaleidoscope.
And the kaleidoscope was a beautiful city,
With colourful light everywhere around it.

And Sarah imagined she is a little princess,
Wherever she went, there would be warriors everywhere.
And she imagined she would live in the city for ever,
But one day it suddenly broke.

She had never been so sad since she was born,
Oh poor little Sarah, oh poor little Sarah.
About two years later she got a new one,
But at that moment she had almost forgotten about
The beautiful *kaleidoscope.*

Catherine Lo (11)
Dame Allan's Girls' School

KALEIDOSCOPE

Looking through a kaleidoscope,
Turn it towards the light:
Lots of patterns and colours you see,
You can't believe the sight.

Looking through a kaleidoscope,
Colours can be seen;
Pink, blue, yellow,
Red, orange and green.

Looking through a kaleidoscope,
Patterns are quite strange.
At every little turn of the end,
The visions shift and change.

Looking through a kaleidoscope,
You won't believe your eyes!
Shapes are dotted everywhere,
Like stars up in the skies.

Lydia Potts (11)
Dame Allan's Girls' School

KALEIDOSCOPIC REALITY

The kaleidoscope is ever changing,
Never the same, colours ranging
From orange to red and blue and green,
So many patterns to be seen.

Funny thing is, it's not really there,
Very pretty to look at and stare.
Yes, but it's a kind of trick,
An optical illusion, ever slick.

Maybe we are like that too,
Never seeing what is true.
Wrapping ourselves up in a fairy tale,
Never seeing children shown as slaves for sale.

Or all the other real scares or frights,
Or all the captives of war, and fights.
It really is quite shocking what you can see,
In kaleidoscopic reality.

Joanna Cantwell (11)
Dame Allan's Girls' School

KALEIDOSCOPE

Please, please, give me a peep!
The word, you know, comes from the Greek:
'Watch beautiful forms' is what it means.
Here they are: red, orange, blues and greens.
Turn the tube and the patterns flow -
Please, please let me have a go.
Yellow, white, pink and blank -
I promise you I'll give it back.

It's not the truth, it's just a trick,
But let me look and I'll be quick:
I'll see the shapes that are changing
Just a turn and they're rearranging.
If you won't share the thing you've shown.
I'll have to get one all of my own.

Fiona Brown (11)
Dame Allan's Girls' School

KALEIDOSCOPE

I see the colours floating by,
Like a multicoloured tie.

Fiery red and russet brown,
Sparkling like a monarch's crown,
Flashing like the clubs in town.

Twist and turn and change the shapes,
See what alters, see what breaks.

Lift it to the light and see,
Patterns revealed in symmetry.

Georgie Kaufman (11)
Dame Allan's Girls' School

CHANGE

Changing,
All the world around us,
Moving,
Every day of our lives;
Seeing,
The shapes that surround us,
Falling and returning,
Different every time.

Different patterns of life:
Not all true;
Illusions, surprises,
Might be waiting for you.
One turn,
One move,
All gone,
So soon.

Tanya Mitra (11)
Dame Allan's Girls' School

KALEIDOSCOPE

See the patterns twirl all around,
Look through the hole where they can be found,
See the pieces of all different colours,
Which make your eyes twinkle with illusions.

Patterns with symmetry and light reflecting
And different shapes ever changing!
Now close your eyes and go to sleep,
Dreaming of colours that you have just seen.

Karis Carr (11)
Dame Allan's Girls' School

KALEIDOSCOPE

Looking through a kaleidoscope
You can see whatever you want
Ever changing like you and the world
With many symmetrical shapes,
It has the colours of the rainbow
And the brightness of the sun
And with its enchanting patterns
I suppose it is like magic to me

Reflections off mirrors make illusions
Things that aren't really there
You can see the way the sea sparkles
And produces waves of all kinds
You can see the fluffy clouds
You can see the soft, falling snowflakes
Melting as they touch the ground,
I suppose it is like magic to me!

Vanessa Pignataro (11)
Dame Allan's Girls' School

KALEIDOSCOPE

Kaleidoscope is one big playtime,
A different pattern with every turn,
With all the colours of the rainbow,
Deep rose, pink, maroon and mist,

There it changes in front of my eyes,
But it's not really there,
It's just a bunch of lies!
Never the same thing . . .
On the kaleidoscope spy.

Anna Gledson (12)
Dame Allan's Girls' School

KALEIDOSCOPE

What can I see?
A beautiful vision,
Glowing before my eyes,
Tiny coloured fragments,
Worthless on their own,
Priceless in their arrangement.
They're trapped in a symmetrical illusion,
Irradiating and illuminating,
In such a special way
They can light up the long dark tube,
Without any fuel or power.
Locked away, behind the lens,
Cerulean, ebony,
Topaz and sapphire,
Terracotta, lilac,
Jade and crimson.
Russet, lapis,
Olive and mauve,
All woven together,
To form an ever changing, optical trick.
I'm definitely glad,
I have eyes,
To see through this . . .
Wonderful kaleidoscope.

Sophie Bauckham (12)
Dame Allan's Girls' School

KALEIDOSCOPE

Look through this into a world of colours
Eyes fixed so hard that they see no others
Most of the colours you see every day
You can see different shapes that turn their own way
Mirrors create the patterns you see
Patterns that look back at me.

Jennifer Moynihan (12)
Dame Allan's Girls' School

KALEIDOSCOPE OF EMOTIONS

You entered, a perfect vision
That much is undeniable,
My eyes with tears,
Streaming,
Revealed the loneliness I once felt,
I was wrong, I know
Now I was wrong,
Forgive me,
I remember all that we had
When I fell, you picked me up
When I lost hope, you regained my faith,
When the door was locked, you were my key.
You're my everything,
You look at me as I once was,
But now I have changed,
And now I know,
You've forgiven me,
And I swear I'll,
Never leave you again.

Zelda Thompson (15)
Kenton School

HALLOWE'EN

The night was cold
The sky was black
I went out with my witch's hat
I travelled the streets
As cold as can be
Where money and candy were given to me
The time got late
The night grew colder
I got a terrible twitch in my shoulder
I then went home and counted my money
All my candy filled a hole in my tummy
Soon the night was over
The hat was put back
Now there is next year and I'm waiting for that.

John Harasym (12)
Kenton School

ALONE

I walked through the wild wood
The slippery path was sodden and slushy
The crippled trees made crazy patterns on the clouds
The miserable moon moved mysteriously through the sky
Big blue spaces to be placed between my eyes
Public places peering . . . not a sound
Blustering leaves over the lonely ground
And night disappears not ever to come round.
Dark comes over the dull, dim light
Hearing the hooting owls in this dark quiet night
Stillness so sacred not even a fright
Flickers of light in the bright moon's light.

Helen Sheppard (12)
Kenton School

THING

Flying round in outer space,
At an incredible pace.
In a flying saucer,
Definitely not a Vauxhall Corsa.
Always cheery,
Never weary.
Some think he's even dreamy,
They never see he isn't like me,
Our alien Lee.
Sometimes we laugh,
Other times we go to the cafe.
A creature from another planet,
With skin as hard as granite.
Oh what a fright it would be,
If people found out he isn't like you or me.

Graeme Simpson (13)
Kenton School

KALEIDOSCOPES

Beautiful colours, shining and glowing
Jumping, moving, swirling, whirling.
Beautiful colours twirling around
Bouncing and bouncing off the
Kaleidoscope ground.

Beautiful shapes, flowers and stars
Brightly coloured beautiful bars.
From a cylinder cone, bright and round,
These beautiful shapes you can see for a pound.

Mellissa Reid (12)
Kenton School

THE TOON ARMY - NEWCASTLE UNITED

Newcastle United are a good team,
and on a good day they can be mean.
Their traditional strip is black and white,
and when in Europe they go on flights.

The fans are great,
and have a lot of faith.
They sometimes go over the top,
and sometimes need a little bop.

Their road to Wembley was quite easy,
but some games were a little squeezy.
When at Wembley versus the gunners,
they sometimes looked like little stunners.

The departure of Keegan,
brought a lot of mixed feelings.
He made a team capable of winning,
and sent a lot of other teams spinning.

The arrival of Kenny,
Didn't spend many pennies.
The performance of him,
ended in the bin.

Then the arrival of Gullit,
was a big bullet.
And that's the story,
of the Toon glory.

Shaun Punton (12)
Kenton School

THE FAN

The fan walks on through this long winter's night,
Only the moon lighting up this cold, frosty sight.
A 2-2 draw, what a game!
That young centre-half is destined for fame.
Now down at the boozer, the TV on,
He sees the strike that made it 2-1.
He orders a pint, he chats to a mate,
He wonders why they kicked off so late.
They talked about the goals and the leaky defence,
And that it was easier to get past than a 1ft fence.
It's 6pm and time to go home,
Before the wife kicks him out on his bum.
He waits at the stop for the 39,
But it doesn't turn up on time.
He arrives home at half-six
And goes in the kitchen to get a Twix.
There he finds to his surprise,
A note that really opens his eyes.
It's from his wife who's finally left him
Because of the football and drinking.
He's not bothered, he doesn't care,
His life's football so there!

Ian Johnson (12)
Kenton School

HALLOWE'EN

If you look up at the sky tonight
You may see something that will give you a fright
She'll have a pointy nose,
A pointy hat,
A broom and a talking cat.
If you don't know what I am talking about now
She'll turn you into a frog somehow.

If you look at the sky another day
The wicked witch will have gone away.
If you would like to see her again
You'll have to go to her kingdom in thunder and rain
Or just be patient wait another year
Because Hallowe'en will soon be here.

Ashleigh Wilks (13)
Kenton School

AUTUMN LEAVES

Autumn leaves are either
red, green or brown.
They are usually found on the ground.
Here, there, anywhere
sometimes in the air.
Changing shape
changing size.
Just like when the sun rises.
Big, small, large, thin
people put leaves in the bin.
Autumn is cold
as people are told.
It's not very nice
it can be like ice.
It might be windy
it might be rainy.
That's what autumn's all about
It's like a roundabout.
Round and round
the seasons go.
But that's autumn, though.

Claire Tait (11)
Kenton School

THE KALEIDOSCOPE

A kaleidoscope is bright,
With its shimmering light.
All different shapes and colours,
I got it off my grandmother.

I can't explain the amazing shape
I wonder who thought of this brilliant make.
Every kid needs one of these,
Instead of buying sweeties.

To have one of these is really cool,
To not have one, you'd be a fool.
A cuddly toy, a remote control car,
No, no, no you must be mad!
A kaleidoscope is really fad.
You'll have lots of fun
If you point it up to the sun.

Now I'm bored with the kaleidoscope bright,
I have a new yo-yo to last me the night.

Natalie Battista (13)
Kenton School

RABBITS, RABBITS, RABBITS

I come in from school
and Mum says
'Philip let the rabbit out'
Then I say 'No need to shout!'

Then my dad says firmly
'Philip clean the rabbit's hutch'
I say to myself
'He thinks he's so butch!'

Then my little brother
with a mouth like a motor
Tells me to change the rabbit's water.

They make me feel
Like a tiny elf,
Then I burst out loud

   'Do it yourself!'   .

Philip Archbold (12)
Kenton School

A KALEIDOSCOPE

Constantly changing patterns
A different breathtaking shape
Each time you view,
But every show begins the same way
Pick up the kaleidoscope and look through.
Constantly altering sentences
A different delightful conversation
Begins anew.
But every friendship begins the same way
Lift up your head to say hello.

What amazing variety
What infinite number of shapes
It's a miracle to look through
The kaleidoscope.
How many time have I wasted
The chance to try again
Because the patterns I've made
With the words I've used
Have not been new.

Rajan Vedhara (11)
Kenton School

ROBERTO CARLOS

R oberto Carlos is the best
O ut of Europe and the rest
B etter than Batty and better than Thuram
E veryone knows his powerful left foot
R oberto Carlos plays defender left
T he whole world knows he is the best
O ut-plays Shearer, Owen and Ba

C urls the ball as fast as a Jaguar
A ches to score the perfect goal
R oberto's feet are magical with a ball
L oves to play for Brazil
O ut of all the teams with his
S kill

Richard Johnson & Vaqas Saleem (12)
Kenton School

KALEIDOSCOPES

I can see it forming as I move it around,
Like magic colours are quickly found.
Red, yellow, orange and blue,
A mirror is pointing straight at you.

A reflection is brilliant, it appears everywhere,
Every time it moves, it seems to tear
Tiny colours each made of glass,
It's a shame that they have to pass.

I see a pattern every time,
I think I can see a spot of lime.
A kaleidoscope is so much fun,
I'm glad it doesn't weight a ton!

Claire Stafford (12)
Kenton School

FIRST DAY BLUES

I was not very far from home
But in the playground on my own.
The building was big, I felt like a twig
I really did want to go home.

At break it was raining outside,
That was a bit of a bind.
Dinner was better, although it got wetter
And I had to stay inside.

But now I'm used to the place,
I haven't got such a long face
I used to be sad, but now I'm glad
I go to Kenton, that's the place.

James Atkinson (12)
Kenton School

KALEIDOSCOPE

Turn the tube to reveal,
Bright colours all around.
Mirrors make these images,
That we are pleased we have found.
Rotate the tube to change the patterns,
Reflecting off a mirror.
Shapes, sizes, colour, as well.
Everything changes at a turn.
To look at these, it is quite fun.
Symmetrical patterns with the colours.
Shake the tube the pattern breaks.
Then turn the tube to begin again.

Laura Waggott (12)
Kenton School

THE TORTOISE

I'm slow and scaly
And known for being lazy
I carry my own home
And live all alone
During the winter I go into hibernation
When I wake up I have a huge celebration
I sleep through the winter until spring
Then I eat the leaves that the children bring.

Kerry Hall (13)
Kenton School

A POEM ABOUT ME

I am very small
But I wish I was tall
I have blonde hair
But sometimes I don't care
I have blue eyes
And I want to wear a disguise
I am kind and sweet
And very petite.

Elaine Burke (12)
Kenton School

KALEIDOSCOPE POEM

Twisting, turning colours,
One after another.
Different shapes and sizes,
Falling into one another.

Hundreds of different patterns,
Sliding down a slope,
Always imaginative,
My colourful kaleidoscope.

Gemma Carr (13)
Kenton School

I Wish I Knew

I wish I knew,
Or somehow could see,
Into the future,
And how we would be.

Happy or sad?
Big or small?
Sane or mad?
Short or tall?

Where would we go?
What would we do?
Who would be there?
A lot or a few?

Where would we live?
Newcastle or Rome?
I don't care,
As it would be home.

If the world was to end,
Would we ever know?
And would our brains stop?

   Yes or no?

Caroline Barrass (12)
Kenton School

HODGSON

H is for hilarious and humorous
O is for owner and obedient
D is for darling and dodging
G is for good and grand
S is for sobs and screams
O is for organised and ordinary
N is for nobody's like him at all.

David Hodgson (13)
Kenton School

KALEIDOSCOPE

Look at that rainbow it's kaleidoscopic
Colours are my favourite topic
Look at those fireworks they are bright
They are at an incredible height
I like flowers that are yellow
Kaleidoscopic means colour you know
Red, yellow, pink and blue
They are all kaleidoscopic colours too!

Danielle Henry (12)
Kenton School

KALEIDOSCOPE

The wind blows,
And the rain flows.
The sun comes out,
And the flowers sprout.
The leaves drop from the trees tall,
And down the snowflakes fall.

Lee Walker (12)
Kenton School

WAITING

In heaven's gate you will be there,
Will you love me, will you care?
I have changed since we last met,
I can't remember, can't forget.

If you'll be there,
I'll wait and see,
Then together you and me.
Before that evil took you away,
I didn't realise and went to play,
I never knew what they had to hide,
But now I know deep inside,
Why they never told the truth,
To protect my innocent youth.

Of the evil adult world,
Was not told, was not learned,
What happened on that worst, worst day,
Was not only your life that was taken away,
But their daughter, sister, cousin, niece,
But what about me? My aunty ceased,
I did not need to know the gory details,
But instead of letting me believe you were still there,
I should have been told,
Didn't they care?
As long as you can care for me,
I'll love you till eternity,
You would have been successful,
You would have been great,
So please wait for me at heaven's gate.

Sarah Layton (16)
Kenton School

THE KALEIDOSCOPE

A kaleidoscope is fun,
amazing and magical.
Look through it and see
spectacular patterns with
little pieces of plastic.
Bright blues, ruby reds,
electric yellows and
Groovy greens.

Turn the top,
Turn it to the right,
Turn it to the left
All the way round it goes!

You feel as though you're
on a different planet then
all of a sudden . . .

Black!

Stacey Santon (12)
Kenton School

KALEIDOSCOPE

Squares and circles
diamond shapes too!
Silver and gold and
yellow and blue.
Butterflies and dragonflies
and a mirrored image.
Looking through the
viewfinder rotating
an *image*.

Michael West (12)
Kenton School

68

A MIST OF COLOURS . . .

When I am tired but cannot sleep,
When I am sad but cannot weep,
I toss and turn and look outside,
Up into the star-filled moonlit sky.

The stars are dotted all around,
And I can hear the whispering sound,
Of the night sky and the morning sun,
Planning what is to be done.

I see shooting stars passing by,
Whispering the night-time lullaby,
The night-time colours - a kaleidoscope,
Fill me with a little hope.

That the sky of night isn't all it seems,
The beautiful stars and shooting beams,
Of happy visions hidden beneath,
The lonely sky of solemn peace.

For when I look in the kaleidoscope sky,
There are pictures in the clouds - no lie,
I see fields of roses, a stormy gale,
The sky is one great fairy tale.

A mist of colours hidden by smoke,
A fairytale kaleidoscope.

Louise Henderson (12)
Kenton School

KALEIDOSCOPE

When I was a very young boy,
I was given a wondrous toy.
A toy with colours, that brought great joy,
I played with it for hours as a boy.

So many colours and different hues,
greens, reds, yellows and many shades of blues.
Changing images at every twist,
magic with mirrors, with a turn of the wrist.

I no longer have my wondrous toy,
but still I live in hope.
That one day soon I will retain that joy.
and get another kaleidoscope!

Jon Rose (12)
Kenton School

KALEIDOSCOPE

Coloured patterns twirling and changing,
Symmetrical sequences forever arranging.
Whirling and swirling, red and green,
Yellow and orange and all colours between,
From imperial purple to dazzling blue,
Transforming shapes of every hue.
Spectacular silver, glimmering gold,
All the colours for you to behold.
Diamonds and circles, triangles and more,
All kinds of shapes for you to explore.
Shapes and colours so hard to cope,
All to be seen in a kaleidoscope.

Eloïse Smith (12)
Kenton School

KALEIDOSCOPE

Looking through the window
Into the darkness,
The world outside
Is in turmoil,
Like a kaleidoscope.

Around you is the sudden snap
Which takes you
To a far-off land
Where the stars gaze down,
And the moon shines so bright
It shines on the trees
With flickers of light,
Like a kaleidoscope.

Shocked by the wind's howl
That seems to be saying,
'Come with me, come.'
You want to step outside
Where the wind is so fierce
It takes the trees in its fists
And shakes them wildly,
Like a kaleidoscope.

Gaze into the fire
Where the flames flicker.
The often crackle
Makes a spark fly,
Like a tiny bird in a storm.
And the candles dance,
Like a kaleidoscope.

Like a kaleidoscope.

Inés Soria (12)
Kenton School

A WINTER'S DAY

I woke up one morning
To open my curtains and see
All the snow was falling
My heart filled with glee!

The trees were all white
The roads were covered in ice
Everything was frozen
But still very nice

I ran to my wardrobe
To pull out my coat
I put it over my jamas
Then a scarf wrapped round my throat

I rushed outside to my garden
To throw a snowball or two
I then built a snowman
Too many things for me to do!

The snow had stopped falling
From the glorious sky
All the snow had melted
As I let out a sigh

I woke up another morning
To open my curtains and see
All the snow was falling
My heart filled with glee!

Laura Mowbray (12)
Kenton School

A FRACTURED VIEW

I woke up on that sunny day,
It was my birthday, the 5th of May.
The air was crisp, the sun was bright,
I hadn't slept all through the night.
I needed to know, what it would be,
My birthday gift from her to me,
I raced downstairs, to see what it was,
I screamed with joy and delight because . . .
The shiny wrapper didn't hide,
The lovely kaleidoscope held inside.
I picked it up and started to boast,
I could see the colours right up close.
The colours made patterns changing every time,
Yellow, red, blue purple and lime.
I didn't let it leave my sight,
Even though my birthday night.
For days and days it was my toy,
The envy of each girl and boy.
One day I decided to take it to school,
I was so stupid, such a fool.
Then Billy snatches it out of my hands,
And I have to watch as it slowly lands,
In little pieces, scattering far and wide,
No teachers there to be on my side.
He runs off, just leaving me there,
With a broken heart and hands that are bare.

Emily Robinson (13)
Kenton School

KALEIDOSCOPE

My kaleidoscope is long and round
With a million colours to astound.

Different shapes and different sizes
Different colours with surprises.

Cathedral windows I can see
And flowers opening up for me.

Costume jewellery flashing bright
Makes me joyful at the sight.

I move my hand and block the light
And all inside is turned to night.

I raise my hand and in comes day
And all the shapes come back to play.

I never tire of peeping in
It makes me smile, it makes me grin.

As silent fireworks whirl and turn
Explosion of colours that never burn.

Parminder Kaur (14)
Kenton School

BILL THE SNOWMAN

Bill the snowman we made him in winter
For his nose we stuck in a splinter
We put him in the back of my garden
At night it's very cold, so we give him a cardigan

He wears a cap and a scarf round his neck
The birds come at dawn and give him a peck
He must be cold out there in the snows
He has seeds for his mouth that's why there are crows

The sun comes out and we all cry
Because we know well - he's going to die
As the day gets hotter and more warm
His cap on the floor and his cardigan torn

The day turns to dusk and he's a puddle
We are in sorrow and our minds are in a muddle
Next year he's going to come back
It's a long time to wait for him and his cap.

Gary Kilday (12)
Kenton School

KALEIDOSCOPE

I see it in the window of the toy shop,
I run in but stop.
I notice something else, I have a quick spy
I put it close to my eye

Pink, orange, white and green
The brightest colours I've seen,
Red, purple, yellow and blue
A few other colours too.

I turn it a little more
And I see a colour I've never seen before.

I put it down in a daze,
And look to see how much money I need to raise,
To buy such a glorious thing,
I didn't have enough,
I couldn't even buy a plastic ring,
So I sent home in a huff!

Julie Armstrong (11)
Kenton School

KALEIDOSCOPE, KALEIDOSCOPE

Kaleidoscope, kaleidoscope,
Unplayed with for years,
Why oh why do you always
Get put under the stairs?

I remember when we were small,
Turning you upside down,
Around and around,
The shapes fascinated us all.

Colours and shapes galore,
Shooting like the stars,
Extremely vibrant yellows,
Like flowers you see in a vase.

Squares, circles and pyramids,
Falling all around,
Reds, blues and purples,
Never making a sound.

You look just like a telescope
To gaze up at the moon,
But then again I really do hope,
To show you off very soon!

Kaleidoscope, kaleidoscope,
Unplayed with for years,
Now that you've been found,
You won't be kept under the stairs!

Victoria Richley (13)
Kenton School

KALEIDOSCOPIC CREATURE

Kaleidoscopic creature,
Came creeping through the dark,
Purple eyes and yellow tail,
With a rainbow-coloured mouth.

Its body was a diamond,
Coloured orange too!
I know you don't believe me,
But honestly it's true.

Its fingers were pink,
Its toes were square,
Its hair was blue,
Oh how I stared.

Kaleidoscopic creature,
Came creeping through the dark,
Its teeth looked like triangles,
And its nose was a star!

It growled at me,
I gasped and jumped,
I was shocked,
What could it be?

Oh kaleidoscopic creature,
Tell me your name
You're blinding me,
With your brightly coloured mane.

Could this be a dream?
No of course it's not,
It's true, please believe me,
I wouldn't say it if it's not.

Lucy Frances Dowey (12)
Kenton School

KALEIDOSCOPE

Twist and turns
Twisting patterns
Lovely patterns
Turning twisting

Made of plastic
Made of glass
Looking lovely
Made at last

Shake again
And watch the mirrors
Turn to the light and you'll see
A rainbow of colours.

Jenna Dargon (12)
Kenton School

WHAT NEXT?

First it's snow and then it's rain,
Drizzling down your windowpane,
The sun is hot, the sky is blue,
Next, what's the weather going to do?
There's a rainbow,
So let it rain more,
The sky is turning grey.
The sun goes in,
The rainbow fades,
The cold air begins to dim.
The frosty ground starts to melt,
The moon comes out.

Claire Redhead (12)
Kenton School

KALEIDOSCOPE

A lot of colours change and change
Making different patterns
Some of them bright
Some of them dull
All in a little tunnel

Looking through a dark thin tunnel
Seeing the colours of the rainbow
First I saw reds
Then I saw blues
Then it went all multicoloured

There was a range of shapes
All put together
I saw green triangles
And orange squares
Then it came to an end.

Jennifer McAvoy (12)
Kenton School

WINTER'S DAY

It was a typical English winter's day
Looking up my mind, was astray
Dark skies and clouds of grey
Changing shape along the way
I saw a dog change into a horse
Just my imagination of course!
Did that car become a plane
Or was I just imagining again?
Back to earth my mind did roam
Time to get up and set off for home.

Stephen Warner (12)
Kenton School

THE SIX FIFTY-FOOT DROP

At last Alton Towers here we are
From Newcastle to Alton we've come quite far
A three hour journey with only two stops
But the sounds are amazing, whacks, bangs, booms and pops.

We rushed to the biggest bestest ride
There are no school rules to abide
The queue was long but we don't care
God it was a hot, sweaty atmosphere.

We talked and we talked as we went around
The steps were taking us about the ground
People were screaming as they went down
Only one hour and a half we'd been queueing now.

We talked and we talked, then talked some more
Now we could actually see the door
Red lights, blue lights, green and more
We were really close to the door.

We were finally strapped in, oh God the din.
We went over then stopped, hovering there
We started falling, we were going that fast
through the smoky hole, it was over, not long did it last.
The ride was over, but it had only just begun!
Well that was my ride on the *Oblivion*.

Julie Smith (14)
Kenton School

RAINBOWS

Look at the rainbow high in the sky
So many pretty colours passing by
Red and yellow, some light green
Orange and blue with indigo too

Rainbows are there after the rain goes
Pity we can't see when the rain falls
If you don't see them, don't make a fuss
Rainbows will be here long after us.

Ashleigh Graham (12)
Kenton School

POLLUTION

The smelly rubbish,
The dirty litter,
The burning cigarette end
The sticky chewing gum,
The crushed beer can,
The empty bin and ripped carrier bags
Why must this be?

The smoky chimneys,
The oily seas, dirty rivers,
The chopped-down trees,
Why must this be?

The smelly streets,
The floating newspapers,
The rolling bottles,
The messy next-door neighbours
Why must this be?

Mountains of litter,
Broken bottles,
Foggy cities with bitter people
Why must this be?

Karl Olsen (12)
Kenton School

THE KALEIDOSCOPIC COLOURS OF THE WORLD

All over the world the colours begin,
to shine and to glow
for us all to see.

They all wake up with a mighty big yawn
ready to glisten
in the hot sun's rays.

As I look out the window
at the morning sky
I am greeted by an illusion of prettiness.

If I go to school or even the park
the colours are there
whether it's light or dark.

Going unnoticed by our unworthy eyes
the colours carry on
their important duty.

To keep this world from a boring end
they shower us with happiness
and their amazing depth.

The natural and the artificial
the pale and the bright
all work together to improve our life.

So please don't forget
the hard work of the colours
that provide us with variety and kaleidoscopic views.

Nina Lowery (12)
Kenton School

HORSES AND PONIES

Riding is such fun to do,
Trotting, cantering and galloping too.
Speeding up the fields and dales,
Bobbing heads and swishing tails.

Then to the stable we shall go,
Getting the horses ready for show.
Brush them,
Groom them,
Plait their mane,
Make sure their stable's clean again.

At the end of the day,
The horse wants to play,
So on the field they run away,
Until tomorrow, another day.

Nicola Grant (12)
Kenton School

KALEIDOSCOPE

K aleidoscopes are a wonderful toy
A must for every girl and boy.
L ovely colours as you can see
E veryone loves it, including me!
I t's beautiful, marvellous and supreme,
D escribing it you'd say it's a dream.
O range is just one colour used
S o many colours, the favourite's hard to choose.
C olours, colours, colours galore!
O h so many colours, they make my eyes sore.
P atterns, patterns swirling around
E veryone look at the new one I've found.

Joanne Shields (11)
Kenton School

FIREWORKS AT NIGHT

Fireworks are dashing
Through the sky at night,
A dazzling galore
Will make you want to see more.

All different colours for you to see
A magnificent range for only 50p.
Lots of little children running round and round
But freezing on the spot when they hear a loud sound.

So if you want to see the fireworks and their luminous rays,
Then buy a ticket to see
Some startling displays.

Amanda Graham (12)
Kenton School

KALEIDOSCOPE POEM

K is for kaleidoscope
A is for all the colours
L is for lovely patterns it makes
E is for every bead
I is for interesting shapes and light
D is for a dazzling sight
O is for optical sight
S is for seeing the patterns
C is for colours which light up your eyes
O is for when you go oh!
P is for people who say it's proper class
E is for the ending of this poem.

Danielle Stafford (11)
Kenton School

CONCERT KALEIDOSCOPE

Pitch black darkness
Nothing to be seen
Then light falls upon us
And a blast of screams

Flashing lights
Bright lights
Coloured lights too
They follow dancers on the stage,
Just for me and you.

Suddenly there's no light
We are haunted by the dark
Glow in the dark costumes being worn
They look like dancing stars.

When the curtain falls
It's the end of the show
The house lights turn on
We wonder how long we'll have to wait for another
Concert Kaleidoscope

Sarah Dowling (13)
Kenton School

KALEIDOSCOPE

Kaleidoscope, a twist and change,
All the colours in the range.
From red to brown,
Brown to blue,
Every twist a golden hue.
Yellow, orange, purple and green,
All the colours I have seen.

Craig Tippins (12)
Kenton School

KALEIDOSCOPE

A toy, a tube
Brightly coloured, glass and mirrors
Reflecting, forming changing patterns.

Twirling, swirling colours
Dancing, moving shapes
A delight to the eye.

Exciting, breathtaking, awesome
Turning, twisting
Dancing before your very eyes.

Patterns changing and repeating
Quick before it changes again
Hurry or you will miss it.

All of these make up a kaleidoscope.

Louise Armstrong (11)
Kenton School

MY KALEIDOSCOPE

Red, green, blue and indigo
The colours seem to come and go
I look, I blink, I move my eyes
Each patterns seems a new surprise
I see them once, they make me squeal
The fun it brings, it must be real
It's getting dark, no more sunbeams
It's torn away my perfect dreams
It's gone away but it's not broke
There's just no light for my kaleidoscope.

Alison Langley (12)
Kenton School

CHRISTMAS NIGHT

I wish today would go away
for tomorrow is Christmas Day
the lights are bright
there's stars tonight
Christmas is great
I really can't wait
tomorrow will come
and it will be done
it started at morning
when I was yawning
I came down the stairs
wearing my flares
the lights were bright red,
black and white
it has already been
that special night.

Jemma Iggleden (13)
Kenton School

KALEIDOSCOPE

Suddenly bits of green,
appear on the screen.
Bright red spots,
then light blue dots.
I hope my eyes can cope
with this kaleidoscope.
Splashes of yellow,
sparkles of pink.
I'm getting a headache
I think!

Shaun Jenkinson (11)
Kenton School

BONFIRE NIGHT

B onfire night is here.
O ohing and aahing as bangers start banging.
N ovember fifth.
F ireworks zooming.
I nfants' excitement fills the air.
R eds and oranges exploding in the dark.
E verybody gazes in amazement.

N othing is dull, everything is bright.
I t's a magical evening.
G uy Fawkes burning at the top of the fire.
H appiness and sadness as the fire dies out.
T hat's all for this year.

Emma Oliver (13)
Kenton School

KALEIDOSCOPE

K aleidoscopes are full of colour
A mber, red, purple and blue
L iving in a world of fantasy
E ach and every day
I n my brown eyes
D ecorations of patterns
O nwards to the future
S lowly as can be
C an't help looking at it
O ption of patterns
P erfect as can be
E ven when I am away.

Long Hoang (13)
Kenton School

KALEIDOSCOPE!

They dance in dark,
They dance in light,
They dance in colours all through the night,

> The stage turns red,
> For blood and pain,
> Then it's green,
> For fresh and clean,

Then black comes for death and sorrow,
The joy is gone, there's no tomorrow,
Minute pass, then yellow shines through,

> Now red, then green, purple and blue,
> The stage is light,
> The costumes dark,
> The colours mix in the lit-up park.

Kathryn Morris & Sarah Nassau (13)
Kenton School

HOPPINGS

The hoppings is a great time of the year,
Some rides are scary and people show their fear,
The waltzer is now my favourite ride,
When I was young it was the giant slide,
I hear lots of different music tunes,
I see out of the ride, comes dark fumes,
I feel that the rain is starting to spit,
But that does not bother me a small bit,
The 'top buzz' spins me round and round
Everything's weird, I cannot hear a sound.

Gary Whitelaw (13)
Kenton School

KALEIDOSCOPE

Look at the deep red sunset,
The sun on its way down,
The explosion of colour
The reds and yellows
The sun is going
Then it's gone.

The moon comes up
Like a silent ghost
Quietly in the sky.

Then in the morning
In the East, far away
The colours explode,
Into the night sky

Breaking the darkness
To bring a new day.

Lynsey Hinshelwood (13)
Kenton School

SEE NOTHING

A sea of blackness, a sky of grey.
A mind full of problems, a tear full of shame.
Not to see, not to glare, all the things I'd miss.
I can't imagine being blind, my life so far from bliss!

A life of doom, a destiny of fear.
A dream of colours, a desire to know.
What do they look like? Do they have a shape?
If colours set the mood, I must be sitting in darkness!

Joanne Loughlin (14)
Kenton School

WORLD CUP

White's of England are playing tonight
Oh what a marvellous sight
Right wing crosses hard and high
Left wing players that money cannot buy
Defenders tackle hard but fair

Captain Shearer a man so rare
Upon the field we play our game
Penalty missed oh what a shame

James Jobson (12)
Kenton School

DISCO

D isco lights are bright
I   ndigo lasers, shining in our sight
S ongs, shapes, and sounds
C olours all around
O range, yellow and green are all the colours that can be seen.

Jimmy Ng & Christopher McDonald (14)
Kenton School

WINTER

Winter is coming and outside the wind is cold.
The snow is falling quietly.
I am upstairs in my bed snug and warm,
My mam is making cocoa.
In the living-room in front of the fire my three dogs are sleeping.
My dad has come in from the cold trying to earn money.

Emma Paxton (11)
Kenton School

KALEIDOSCOPE

How does it feel
Not to be able to see
Turquoise or fuchsia pink?
Not to know about
The green of spring,
Or the hot yellow of summer?
What about autumn?
Not to see
The browns and reds
Or the icy
Blue of winter?
Not to know what gold is,
Or to see a beautiful sunset.
How does if feel
Not to dream
About flowers,
Or trees?
Not to see.

Gillie Kleiman (14)
Kenton School

EURO 96

I remember the colours of Euro 96
When I went to see the games,
the Romanians and Bulgarians all
playing drums and cheering names.

All the flags, reds, yellows and blues,
oranges, greens and whites too,
I remember Stoichkov scoring a goal
from a free kick outside the box.

I saw Wembley on the TV
the colours there were extraordinary,
St George's crosses waving around
Sun hats being thrown to the ground.

I remember crying at the semi final
I had become very sad
but then I looked back and thought
What colourful weeks I'd had.

Daniel Sanderson (13)
Kenton School

KALEIDOSCOPE

Looking into a colourful tube,
There are colourful beads,
Making colourful patterns,
They are colourful flowers,
Colourful roses
And colourful bluebells,
Colourful fuchsias
And colourful foxgloves.

Looking into a colourful tube
There are colourful beads,
Making colourful patterns:
Red
And green
And blue
And yellow.

Looking into a colourful tube
There are colourful beads,
Making colourful patterns.

Eleanor Parkin (13)
Kenton School

KALEIDOSCOPE
CHRISTMAS

The lights from the tree make you pretty glad,
The colours all around you aren't that bad.
The wrapping from the presents consist of many colours,
You're feeling nice and warm when you jump up from the covers.

The brightness of the colours, the one that is snow,
It really makes your eyes light up and then they start to glow.
The cards pinned up upon the walls
And the shining from the tree are the things called baubles.

Christmas crackers red, green and gold,
Remind us of the Christmases of new and of old.
And once again the best of all that fall from high to low,
The patterns and the crumples of the deep, deep snow.

Sean Graham (13)
Kenton School

FIREWORKS

I stand staring up into the black of the
night . . . waiting.
Soon I hear long whistles of small rockets zipping,
zooming, I still stand staring . . . waiting.
Suddenly the sky is bright with explosions of colour
and light.
Flashes and sprays of multicoloured-coloured stars,
purple, green, yellow, so bright,
purple orange with a hint of white.
I am no longer waiting.

Amy Syron (14)
Kenton School

A WALK IN THE PARK

A walk in the park, the sky not very dark.
I look up to the tree and it looks up to me.
I see a kaleidoscope of colours churning and mixing
through the silhouette of the setting summer sun.

The crisp golden brown leaves rustle past my feet
jumping and crackling in the autumn wind.
I see the colours of transparency and still turquoise
trickle past me in the form of the stream.
The sunbeams reflecting off the still parts of the water
make the area seem so tranquil and peaceful on the calm
autumn evening.

It's amazing what you can see on a walk in the park!

Christopher Taylor (13)
Kenton School

KALEIDOSCOPE

Kaleidoscope of colour and light
All is reflected clear and bright
Lots of patterns constantly change
Evolving into different shapes
I am transfixed
Dancing colours mixed
Orange, red, yellow and green
Stare at the colours on the screen
Constantly changing shapes and colours
Of these there is one that I watch
Paralysed by the beauty
Ending on just my colour, one little blue star

Michael Heenan (13)
Kenton School

A NIGHT AT THE HOPPINGS

We get off the train
And walk over the field
I promise I'll not scream
I'll keep my lips sealed.

We go on the rides
And spinning all about
We get even faster
I scream and I shout

The dazzling colours
Are shining so bright
Everything is perfect
Here on this warm night.

Kimberley Duffy & Tracey Goscombe (13)
Kenton School

KALEIDOSCOPE

The lights flash as I dance,
I watch and look while I prance,
My stardust shines in the hall,
I look up at the glittering ball,
The starship trooper searches,
And then it suddenly pounces,
So I dance,
Glittering suits moving about,
Dancing to an electric flute,
Blue and red seem to shine,
Painting images from time to time.

Gareth Evans (13)
Kenton School

KALEIDOSCOPE

The bright colours,
The symmetrical patterns,
The colours of the rainbow all mixed in one.
The reflection of the shapes,
The cracks in the mirrors,
They make you see double.
The infinite patterns,
You could spend all day trying to make different patterns,
But there will always be one,
You will never know.
The shapes are amazing,
The angles, the colours.
Diamonds, squares, triangles,
It's got them all.

Michael Rankin (13)
Kenton School

A MIXTURE OF TIME

As I walk through the woods of my life,
Bearing all including strife,
I am oblivious to the mixture of time,
Greens turn to reds, reds go to yellow,
The brown has to follow,
The brown shrivels up,
Like a little paper cup,
Then falls to the floor,
As I watch in awe,
I have realised of course it is the autumn years of my life,
In its own mixture of time.

Richard Aldred (13)
Kenton School

KALEIDOSCOPE

The kaleidoscope is a tube like thing which changes
colours, oh what joy it brings,
Red, yellow, blue, green.
The prettiest colours you've ever seen.
Hold it up to your eye and turn it round,
Watch the patterns change without making sounds.
The kaleidoscope is a magical device,
Which makes you happy, turns bad things nice.
How many colours can you see?
Ten, twenty, thirty maybe!
Colours and patterns mixed up together,
Use your kaleidoscope forever and ever.
It's strange to think that this colourful toy could enchant
your mind, boy oh boy.
That's all I can say about a kaleidoscope right now,
Pretty colours and shapes.
Wow.

Anna Tweddell (13)
Kenton School

MICHAEL OWEN

Owen, Owen is his name, come and
    watch him play the game.

When he has the ball he will score
    plenty of goals.

Eighteen years old and he plays for
    England scoring goals, winning games.

Next to a hero Alan Shearer, what a dream
    playing with him.

Joseph Scott & Peter Macmillan (11)
Kenton School

A MONSTER HARVEST

Humans have their fruit and veg,
fresh and ripe and green.
But the weird things at the monster feast,
Are the grossest that you've ever seen!
So take a breath and hold your nose,
and wash your fingers clean . . .

Cesspit creatures caked in grime,
Rotten, slippery festering slime,
All these things are thought the best
at the annual monster feast.
Now we think we've got a hunch,
that we've put you off your lunch!

Bleeeaaarrgh . . .

Linzi Wheatley & Stacey Wait (11)
Kenton School

KALEIDOSCOPE

Colours and shapes everywhere,
turn it again if you dare.
A colourful rainbow in the sky,
a million colours passing by and by.
The light and mirrors make the colours reflect,
into your eyes the colours inject.

The changing patterns make no sound,
but the shapes inside go round and round.
You'll never see the same pattern again,
forever lasting, there is no end.

Vicki Gray (12)
Kenton School

COLOURS COME FROM EVERYWHERE

Colours here
Colours there
Colours come
from everywhere.

In the rainbow
They will sit
Until the time
reaches five or six.

Now it is the
last moment to
see the colours
before everything
goes dark and
darker until there
is nothing left.

Lisa Appleby (11)
Kenton School

KALEIDOSCOPE

Colours swirling round and round,
They make me totally spellbound,
Falling shapes everywhere,
Look at that one over there!
Diamonds, squares, triangles too,
Lots of shapes for me and you!
A tube lined with mirrors,
Symmetrical patterns, stars and light,
It's like a gorgeous starry night!

Sarah Bolland (13)
Kenton School

KALEIDOSCOPE

All different colours,
All different shapes,
All different patterns,
That the kaleidoscope makes.

Some are round,
Some are square,
Colours and shapes,
Are everywhere.

Blues and greens,
Shades of white,
Yellow and pinks,
To make patterns bright.

Emma Hutton (12)
Kenton School

KALEIDOSCOPE

The pretty colours.
The symmetrical patterns and rainbow of colour.
The streams of blues, yellows, greens and reds,
They go on forever, the patterns are infinite.
The mirrors make it all the more fascinating,
The colours bounce off each other.
The colours, patterns and styles jump out and grab you,
The colours trying to escape,
You need sunglasses to prevent them.
Diamonds, squares, circles and triangles,
This is a kaleidoscope.

Nicholas Allan (12)
Kenton School

SUMMER DAYS

When I think of summer days,
That is when I start to gaze.
To gaze at the bright blue sky
And that is when I start to sigh.
The sun shines brightly as can be,
But the sun will always shine on me.

In the summer, flowers bloom,
You take away dead leaves with a broom.
The smell of barbecues in the air,
Makes you wish that you were there.
Here I sit in the sun,
Watching everyone having such fun.

When we come to the end,
While I'm playing with my friend.
So this is the end of my poem,
Now you can all go home.

Nicola Burnell (11)
Kenton School

KALEIDOSCOPE

Many tiny pieces,
Falling into place.
The light shines through the lens,
As you hold it to your face.

Lots of different colours,
Moving all around.
You can look through it for hours,
Though it makes no sound.

Greens, yellows, reds and blues,
It is magic to your eyes.
Every pattern's different,
So it takes you by surprise.

Kaleidoscopes are special,
They are one of a kind.
Just twist the cap upon the end,
And see what you can find.

Christina Gray (12)
Kenton School

THE KALEIDOSCOPE

A present for my birthday,
I wonder what it is.
Wow!
It's amazing.

There's a fantasy of colours,
There's a fantasy of shapes,
There are lots of different patterns
that lie deep within.

It's like a shattered mirror,
In thousands of little bits,
It's like lots of little stars
glittering in the sky.

We'll never be able to see,
All the patterns deep within.

It's a clever little thing!

Danielle Jegier (12)
Kenton School

KALEIDOSCOPES

Kaleidoscopes are full of colour,
Colour they are.
Are they just a dream,
Or reality?
I don't know what they are?

Please,
Kaleidoscope oh, kaleidoscope,
What are you?
With your colours floating around,
Are you a . . .
Telescope with different colours?
Or maybe just a plain old . . .
Kaleidoscope

Emily Kasher (12)
Kenton School

KALEIDOSCOPE

Lots of colours
Red, white and blue
Colours for me
Colours for you
Lots of shapes
All different sizes
Turn the wheel
For more surprises.
Reflecting rainbows
Into my head
Then stars and stripes
Are there instead.

Jonathan Heron (13)
Kenton School

CHRISTMAS

C hristmas is a festival of joy and also we remember
   the birth of Jesus Christ.
H appy Christmas are the words everyone says when
   they get up on Christmas morning.
R eady, steady, go, when these words are said everyone
   starts to open their presents.
I have to ring my grandmother and what a shock she gets
   when everyone shouts Merry Christmas into the telephone.
S isters, mums, and dads give presents to everyone, that is the
   delight, giving presents to each other.
T ogether all of the family have their turkey dinner.
M um got a bottle of perfume, dad got a shaving kit,
   everyone gets a present off me for Christmas.
A new year is on its way, but first we have Christmas Day.
S o that's it, Christmas is over, but we still have New Year yet!

Laura Patterson (11)
Kenton School

KALEIDOSCOPE

Yellow, blue, green and red,
All these colours in my head.
Look through the hole to see
the pattern, beautiful: a bit like satin.
Point it up to the light,
Colourful stars at night.
all colours, all shapes,
All patterns the kaleidoscope makes.
The diamonds and jewels are really cool,
If you look through this you are no fool.

Adelle Bohill (12)
Kenton School

KALEIDOSCOPES

I collided with a kaleidoscope one day,
I saw funny shapes,
That knocked me for six,
I couldn't understand it.

I looked right in,
What did I see?
Funny old shapes,
That's what I see.

I turn it around,
Quite amazing I say.
I say it again and again,
Brilliant.

I walk with it
Stumbling all over,
Walking left, right
All over the place.
Kaleidoscopes.

David Graham (12)
Kenton School

KALEIDOSCOPE

Rainbow colours
Majestic patterns
Never ending
Forever different

Patterns 'til
The end of time
Safe in plastic
Stuck inside

Light peeps inside
Through a pinhole
Bounces off mirrors
To my eye

Symmetrical patterns
Always changing
Colours and shapes
Strangely addictive

Charlotte Clarke (12)
Kenton School

KALEIDOSCOPE

It's like a star-filled dream
Colours great and small
Diamonds, squares and many more
All coming at you, through one tube

It's like a star-filled dream
Infinite patterns, colours galore
All so bright and colourful
All coming at you, through one tube

It's like a star-filled dream
Reflecting mirror, all galore
Possible patterns all go past you in one flash
All coming at you, through one tube

It's like a star-filled dream
It is a kaleidoscope
All coming at you, through one tube

Christopher Scragg (13)
Kenton School

KALEIDOSCOPE

It's like a rainbow, so soft, sweet, and colourful
Colourful shapes, all different sizes and patterns
Patterns go on forever, they look so soft and warm
Warm colours surround my eyes when I look down the tube
Tube filled with mirrors that create the right effect
Effects of the shape make it worth looking through.

Through the hole in the tube of my
Kaleidoscope

Emma Thomas (13)
Kenton School

KALEIDOSCOPE

Kaleidoscope is a tube.
Kaleidoscope is a mirror.
Kaleidoscope has shapes.
Kaleidoscope is fun to play.
Kaleidoscope you can play all day.
Kaleidoscope has colours.
Kaleidoscope makes patterns.
Kaleidoscope rotates and changes shapes.
Kaleidoscopes are the best.

Keith Rowell (13)
Kenton School

KALEIDOSCOPE POEM

A sparkling brightness,
In your eyes,
An incredible likeness,
To the skies.

It's just a telescope,
In disguise,
But you couldn't tell that,
With your eyes.

Christopher Healy (13)
Kenton School

KALEIDOSCOPE

I see things here, I see things there,
many shapes, many sizes
and all of them big surprises.
Colours change from light to bright,
some big, some small.
There are so many
you cannot focus on them all.
It is a gift to walk through
and now I do not feel so blue.

Lisa Fay (12)
Kenton School

KALEIDOSCOPE

Kaleidoscopes
are like life.
Ever-changing patterns,
different every day,
in a certain sort of way.
Twist the end and it'll soon mend
all the gloom in your room.

Stuart Carey (11)
Kenton School

KALEIDOSCOPE

K aleidoscopes,
A re full of exciting
L ovely patterns,
E legant shapes reflect off the mirrors,
I love *kaleidoscopes*
D elightful colours
O btuse angles make it easy to
S ee the symmetrical
C olourful shapes
O ctagons, triangles,
P arallelograms are just some of the
E xciting, intriguing shapes.

Mark Eaglesham (13)
Kenton School

KALEIDOSCOPE

Light and glass,
Reflect like rainbow.
Incessant in infinite.
Patterns are possible.

All shapes and sizes.
Colours call
'Orange, yellow.'

Kaleidoscopes,
Colours like the rainbow.
Mirrors make it glow.
It's bright with a pretty sight.

Samantha Morley (12)
Kenton School

LIFE IS LIKE A KALEIDOSCOPE

Life is like a kaleidoscope,
the world is a mass of colours.
Everyday reflects the last,
we follow the same old pattern.
Life is like,
a kaleidoscope.

We'll never see all the colours,
or feel all the emotions,
we'll never solve all our problems.
But I hope just once we could stop,
being a kaleidoscope.
And solve all the problems that are in this dear old world.

Samantha Selby (12)
Kenton School

KALEIDOSCOPE

Kaleidoscope is what it's called,
An exciting toy to behold.
Light shines into the tube,
Eyes that look in wonder,
Inside mirrors do the trick,
Dancing the shapes around,
Oblong, squares and diamonds,
Shapes of all different sizes,
Colours cascading back and forth,
Orange, red, blues and greens.
Patterns that are beautiful,
Entrancing you for hours.

Jane Worthington (12)
Kenton School

KALEIDOSCOPE

Looking down the long, round tube,
What colours do you see?
The shapes and patterns go on forever,
Like a rainbow sea!

The incessant shapes and colours,
Fill the enlightened tube.
All the shapes under the sun,
Shapes like diamonds and cubes!!!

The symmetrical patterns,
The mirrors inside reflect!
Like stars in the sky at night,
Into your eyes inject!!!

Stare at the colours,
Try to look beyond . . .
You'll see the little beads,
Every single one!!!

Amy-Jade Osman (13)
Kenton School

KALEIDOSCOPE!

Twisting, turning every way
like leaves falling from a tree
on an autumn day.
Colours blind you by sight
taking you to your wildest
dreams by night.

Sarah Cartner (11)
Kenton School

KALEIDOSCOPE

Kaleidoscopes are long round toys
Lovingly played with by girls and boys.
Take a look in the peephole to see what you find,
Colours and shapes of every kind.

Red, yellow, green and blue
Are colours waiting just for you.
With circles, triangles and even squares,
When you look in the peephole you'd better beware.

Once it's picked up, you can't put it down,
You turn the base around and around.
Just make sure it won't get you dizzy,
And your brothers and sisters don't get in a tizzy.

Joseph Tait (13)
Kenton School

KALEIDOSCOPE

The colours in a kaleidoscope can usually be quite cool.
The shape of the kaleidoscope is usually a tube.
Red and yellow, blue and green -
these are the colours in this fantastic machine.
Round and around the lens it turns,
all primary colours for young ones to learn.
Make sure you point it directly to the light
as the colours respond better with white.
You can get a lot of fun out of a kaleidoscope.
Just make sure you use it right
as it really is such a delight.

Leona Bannon (13)
Kenton School

KALEIDOSCOPE

Yellows, red, greens and lots of different shapes are some of
the things a kaleidoscope makes.
Look through the hole and see the patterns,
Some are thin and some are splattered.
I can never get bored with it because it's properties are infinite.

Kayleigh Scott (12)
Kenton School

CHRISTMAS SURPRISES

Christmas is vibrant, enthralling and fun,
Christmas is exciting for everyone.
The climate is freezing,
It feels below minus-nought.
There should be snowmen everywhere,
Well that's what I thought.
The snowflakes are now falling, falling gently to the ground,
There are children playing all around.
I don't want Christmas to be over, never, ever, ever.
I want it to be every day and go on forever.

Every home is decorated, finished with a tree,
Everyone is happy, happy as can be.

Christmas is the day when Jesus was born.
Christmas is the day when wrapping paper is torn.
People enjoy Christmas because they share it with family and friends.
You and me hope that Christmas will never end.

Christmas is nearly over,
Christmas is nearly done,
We will have to pack away and wait for the next one.

Nikita Allan (12)
Killingworth Middle School

SCHOOL

School is good it can be cool
But there are lessons that make me drool.
Art is good, music is boring,
When I'm in history I'm always yawning.
I like French, it is great
But it can be hard to concentrate.
Experiments make an ugly mess,
That's science for you at KMS.
Geography drives me around the bend,
I feel like escaping in a Mercedes Benz.
I like maths it is exciting
But things like algebra can be frightening.
English can also be great,
RE is that thing that I really hate.
So school has its ups and downs,
If we don't go there we'll be as thick as clowns.

Daniel Wombwell (13)
Killingworth Middle School

WINTER

Snowflakes glide through the night
shining in the bright starlight.
As they trickle on the frosty ground
they don't make one single sound.
The floor looks like a polar bear
with long and soft and furry hair.
But inside it is quite warm
for I am protected from that storm.

Laura Gillie (12)
Killingworth Middle School

THE NOOMAGENS

It was the 8th June 1981
8.00 pm and the sun was gone.
From the sky came something the size of my house,
I scampered across the garden like a little, scared mouse.
The chrome door opened at the speed of light,
A purpose thing stood there as dark as the night.
His eyes were the size of my palms,
I was shaking inside but I tried to keep calm.
I said, 'Why are you here?'
'We've come from Noomag, to check inside of your ear.'
Then he hurried into his ship,
It rose in the air and then began to dip.
Then came another ten,
I never saw them, ever again.

Mark Donnelly (13)
Killingworth Middle School

MY PUPPY PEPPER

I have a playful puppy called Pepper,
she'll eat bacon and eggs if I let her.
She tears round my house like a hooligan,
she needs to go to dog school again.
She licks my face and looks up my nose,
there's a hole in my slipper and she chews on my toes.
She's really soft like a teddy bear,
she smells of dog food but I don't really care.
I still love her.

Terence Morgan (12)
Killingworth Middle School

MY ANIMALS

My dog is black, as black as the sky,
A deep brown colour is that of its eyes.
It has got a silk-like coat,
And it cost us a lot of notes!
It's worth it though because it's cute,
It's worth more to me than an Armani suit.

My cockatiel is grey,
A lot of words it can say.
Sunflower seeds are its favourite food,
And it's never in an unhappy mood.
Sometimes when out it will excrete,
On the carpet though but not on a seat.

My fish is gold,
And slippery to hold.
It has healthy teeth and bones,
And all day it grinds on stones.
It wafts its way through the water,
Circling around as if in a rota.

James Bailey (13)
Killingworth Middle School

FUN HOLIDAYS

Holidays are great fun.
Mum relaxes in the sun.
We play volleyball, we always lose.
Mum shouts, 'I'm having a snooze!'
James and me have a game of pool.
Boys drool, girls are cool!
We jump in the pool we make a splash.
Dad jumps in we all better dash.

Emma Good (12)
Killingworth Middle School

MY TRADITIONAL CHRISTMAS

Suddenly, it's Christmas Eve.
I'm very excited,
it's snowing outside.
Everyone is making snowmen
and having snowball fights.
My dad is preparing the dinner,
my mam is making sure the decorations are up.
Me and my sister are out in the snow playing games,
having fun
but now it's bedtime.
We take our wet clothes off
Christmas Day, *yippee!*
All the colours flash before our eyes.
We open our presents
It's so exciting
Later we have a lovely dinner,
and my mum, dad, sister, grandma, granda and I
we sit down and relax,
to watch the Christmas programmes on TV.
It is a very exciting day.

Lauren Muir (13)
Killingworth Middle School

MY FISH

The golden scaly skin of my fish
shining brightly in the water
around his goldfish infested water.
At the top flaky food floats on the water.
He turns at every little sound,
and there's a little splash in the water.

Daniel Shaw (12)
Killingworth Middle School

BODY BITS

Feet are for standing, running and walking.
The mouth is for eating, kissing and talking.
Ears are for hearing the birds in the sky,
and to stop your hat falling over your eyes.
Eyes are for crying and filling with tears,
also for seeing, thanks to your ears.
Hair is for combing and cutting with shears
and for covering over sticky out ears.
Elbows and knees they all come in pairs,
give terrible pain when banged on tables and chairs.
There's no end of trouble and misery caused,
smashing again into half-open doors.
Then there's the neck, well what can I say?
It stops your head falling off, so I think that's OK.
The smell of curry, the scent of roses,
This is why we need our noses.
Aromas from the cooking meat,
and the smell that wafts from my brother's feet.

Jenny Foggo (12)
Killingworth Middle School

LOVE IS IRREPLACEABLE

Love is a flower, love is a rose.
Without love we wouldn't be the same.
Love is an angel flying through the sky.
Love is a white dove sitting in the tree.

Love is when your heart pounds,
Love is when the bells ring.
Love is irreplaceable.
We can't live without love.

Lisa Marchbanks (12)
Killingworth Middle School

THE BEST INTERNATIONAL BAND

I think they are the best international band,
It was just Louis Walsh who gave
them a hand.
Three albums and loads of singles too,
just listen it's like they're singing to you.
When they started they were quite small time,
when they were interviewed they stood in line.
Four of them went through straight away,
the fifth was picked another day.
They have loads of money, they spend it
on clothes,
and holidays in the sun.
They are never off their mobile phones,
they are the best band in the world.
Yes, you guessed it, they are
Boyzone!

Jacqueline Law (13)
Killingworth Middle School

CHRISTMAS

Snow is feathery and smooth
it gets so deep you can hardly move.
Snowman making everywhere.
Candles burning down and down.
Flashing lights control my mind.
The angel at the top of the tree winks at me.
The stockings on the fireplace
will soon be full of grace.
The tree is sparkling with the bright lights
and I am sick of these dark nights.

Amy Skinner (12)
Killingworth Middle School

SUMMER HOLIDAYS

All the tiring work has passed,
and now I have six weeks to last.
I can now lie back and rest,
like a bird in its nest.
The climate boiling,
friends grow annoying.
The sweat is running down us all,
in the stillness there's no breath at all.
Later on we go to a special celebration
but I don't think there is an occasion.
We all had a summer romance,
with some lush lads from Paris, France.
When they left we got their address,
it's hard to read, it's a terrible mess.
Altogether, my holidays were great,
we had such fun me and my mate.

Stephanie Lawrence (13)
Killingworth Middle School

THE WEATHER CONTEST

The rain has failed the contest,
Here's the thunder,
Thinking it's best.
Snowflakes were far too soft
And the cloudy sky has got lost.
Who will win this contest?
We want to know who is best.
Altogether they are dull.
So the best is the sun,
It has won.

Rachel Glass (12)
Killingworth Middle School

THE SEASIDE OF MY IMAGINATION

Strolling over the sandy strands,
wondering, waiting, 'What is there?'
I can hear the roar of the waves,
As they crash up against the cliffs.
I walk a bit further it hits me,
the smell of the sea salt as well as clean air.
I stand there not moving an inch
cold and wet in the icy rain of spray.
I can see the sea as deep and as dark
as the ocean ahead.
It's amazing just watching the crabs
scuttle up and down the beach
grabbing fish that have been abandoned by the sea.
All those shells with all the different colours which sparkle.
This I hope will be the seaside of the future.
Not just the seaside of my imagination.

Gillian McDougal (12)
Killingworth Middle School

SNOWFLAKES

The snowflakes whirl around you,
they're so soft and delicate.
They glide down individually
landing without a thud.
Some fall on to you gracefully.
You run inside looking at
your coat, hat and gloves.
You stare them up and down
but as if by magic the snowflakes are gone.

Rhiannon Clark (12)
Killingworth Middle School

MOTHER NATURE'S WORLD

It comes roaring through the valleys,
It deluges from the skies.
Sometimes it's white and sparkly,
It changes in front of your eyes.

Angry thunder booms over your head,
If lightning strikes your body, you'll be very dead.

Mother Natures rules,
She cannot be defeated,
If you even tried it
You'd be history being repeated.

It comes roaring through the valleys,
It deluges from the skies.
Sometimes it's white and sparkly,
It changes in front of your eyes.

If Mother Nature is defeated
What challenges have we left?

Andrew Clyde (12)
Killingworth Middle School

CANDY THE FOAL

Candy is like snow on a winter day
Candy is lovely in every way.
Candy's eyes are big and bright
in the darkness of the night.
Candy's fur is as smooth as silk
Candy drinks loads of her mother's milk.

Holly Barber (13)
Killingworth Middle School

ARCADE

The games I'm afraid,
are not very cheap.
Pull out your money,
Oh what a big heap.
Coppers change,
last week's sweets.
Nimble hands and
dextrous feet.
My hands are shaking,
my feet are bent.
The way I am going,
my money is almost spent.
The air is alive,
with the smell of hot chips.
My tummy is rumbling,
I'm licking my lips.
I'm faced with a dilemma,
It's really quite sad.
I've got 80p left,
things are looking really bad.
The choice is quite obvious,
it's the bandit or chips.
I must choose one or the other
as I'm licking my lips.
I've made a decision,
I put 20p in the slot.
I push the red button
and I've won the *Jackpot.*

Peter Marshall (12)
Killingworth Middle School

THE FEELINGS OF ANGER

Anger is a feeling,
Depending on your mood,
If you possess a bad temper,
It can result in being rude!
Everything seems to annoy you,
You dive into storms of rage,
People would think you're an animal
Who should be locked tight in a cage,
You can't seem to smash enough things,
Eventually you do calm down
Still you'd like to carry on
But you've broken everything around.
So you're sitting on the floor,
When the last pricey ornament falls,
Then you realise to yourself,
It was nothing to be mad about at all.

Haylee Watson (13)
Killingworth Middle School

IT'S ALL BLACK

The biggest mystery in the world is space,
Out of everywhere it's the biggest place.
When you take off you will be alright,
Just try to dodge the satellites.
And another thing, when you're up there
it can be quite fun,
remember to avoid obstacles like the sun.
So if you have enough money to buy a ship,
I'll tell you this, you're in for a trip.

Luke Bailey (12)
Killingworth Middle School

HOMEWORK RULES OK?

I sacrifice my life today,
To all this work and no play.
I like school it's not all that bad,
Just the homework makes me sad.
Education is like a football game,
For each party it's never the same.
The time I spend night after night,
Racking my brains to get it right.
The golden rule is to knuckle down,
Put the work in now and you'll be sound!
My mam complains about presentation,
Does she really understand the situation?
I'm not allowed to eat or play,
Until the homework rule's obeyed.

Richard Marshall (12)
Killingworth Middle School

WINTER - A COLD DAY OF FUN

It is very cold outside,
We have to wear woolly jumpers and things like that.
Never what we want to wear,
Sometimes we build snowmen, and we make snowballs
and then start to throw them at people.
Big or small, doesn't matter what size,
as long as they don't hit the eyes.

Most of the time we play on sleighs,
going as fast as we can.
Once we nearly crashed into a tree.
We also decorated our sleighs
with tinsel and baubles, we even added a fairy.

Robert Moy (12)
Killingworth Middle School

AT THE BEACH

We're at the beach having fun,
My little brother is playing with his gun.
We run in the water and make a splash,
He is on for chase, I better dash.
We go for a hot dog and sit in the sand,
After we finish here come the band.
The water is still and very calm,
I know the fish will do no harm.
Together we walk past lots of rock pools,
There are lots of crabs, how cool.
The sky above is very blue,
Who's on for hide and seek? You?
The sand is yellow just like the sun,
Ahh! There's a crab, we better run.
Now we're going home, 'cause it's getting late,
When we get there, I'll pick another date.
I'm looking forward to going again.

Kayleigh McNamara (12)
Killingworth Middle School

RADICAL RODENT

My hamster's stupid, I should say mad,
He's very adventurous and always bad.

He's a bit plump, a heavy lump,
And when he's not fed, what a grump.

So the other day he looked a bit creased,
So I gave him an iron, now he's deceased.

Yesterday I asked for another pet,
But my dad said to me, 'Not yet.'

Christopher Porter (12)
Killingworth Middle School

MOTOR ACTION

Screeching round the corners, one hundred miles an hour.
Tearing down the straights, three hundred brake horsepower.
Into the corner, on the ragged edge,
If you lose control you'll go flying through the edge.
Into the pit for some new tyres,
While I am waiting the leader flies by us.
Down with the jacks, wheels spin away,
You come flying out, the crowd shout, 'Hooray.'
In the commentary box everyone's excited,
I catch up to the leader, the pit crew are delighted.
I see the yellow flags fly past.
Someone's crashed going far too fast.
Five laps of yellow flags, no overtaking no one dare pass.
It feels as if I am going so slow, like driving on the grass.
I see the green flag in front of me.
I whiz past the leader like a demented bee.
First in the corner, first back out.
I am going to win now, there's no doubt.
I see the famous flag, chequered black and white.
I cross the line first what a delight.
In the winner's circle
In first place.

Terry Moor (12)
Killingworth Middle School

VISIONS IN MY MIND

As I stood and watched on a cold wintry night,
I saw a little shadow in the moonlight.
My knees began to tremble,
My heart skipped a beat,
I wonder what that shadow was sitting on that seat?

Then I felt a cold breeze running by my side,
I didn't know what it was, then opened up my eyes,
And then I realised what it was,
It was nothing so unkind,
It was just my imagination playing with my mind.

Kirsty Fletcher (12)
Killingworth Middle School

MY DOG (SAM)

My dog Sam is very gentle
I throw a stick and he goes mental.
When he gets a soapy bath
He looks as though he's going to laugh.

When we first got our dog Sam
He was sad to leave his mam.

When it's time for him to eat
He will sit at my feet,
And when he sits at my feet,
I will say 'Do you want to eat?'

I'll get up and make his lunch,
He will have a meaty munch.

You will have to watch your dinner,
Or soon you'll be a lot thinner.
He likes to chew on my slippers,
Anyway, where are my slippers . . .
Sam!

Michael North (12)
Killingworth Middle School

THE DRAMATIC CUP FINAL

'Gripping stuff in this Cup Final'
The commentator said, high up in the ground.
'Tied at 0-0 with five minutes to go,
And listen to the fans' chants going around!'
'Play up now, Owen!' and 'More power, Shearer!'
They're loyal supporters, I think you'll agree.
A dramatic Cup Final, but, as of yet,
Nobody's scored, they can't find the goal-key!
But here's Owen now, he's wearing all red,
A delicate flick, but no, it's just wide.
As we head now for extra time,
So get set for a sensational ride!
Two minutes left, Shearer has a try,
On target! On target! It's going in!
No it's not, Owen has saved the day,
It's gone out of play, and into the bin!
The colourful crowd, just over two thousand
Watched from the sidelines, the final showdown.
Some wore scarves, some wore bobble-hats, most of them had rattles
And one of them dressed like a clown!
'A chance now, for Owen!' the commentator said.
'He's made contact! It's good! It's going up . . .
Shearer's missed it, *it's in!* And Billy Owen
Has won this year's National Tiddlywinks Cup!
Lennie Shearer collects his loser's medal,
But cries of joy as Owen lifts up the prize!'
So you thought it was a football match then?
Sorry, that was a big pack of lies!

Stuart Burns (13)
Killingworth Middle School

HOLIDAYS

Holidays are fun,
Wherever you may go,
They are really enjoyable,
Even if it starts to snow.

It can be really scorching,
Or maybe freezing cold,
It might even be exciting,
Excitement makes you bold.

You sit there on the beach,
Catching some sun rays,
And you smile just thinking,
How much you love these summer days.

The beach is packed full,
It's filled up to the brim,
There's people in the turquoise sea,
I might go for a swim.

Later on it will be dark,
I'd better get home soon,
I want to sit up in my lodge,
And watch the stars and moon.

Sitting in my lodge,
Made of wood and stuff,
I will go to bed now,
I think I've had enough.

Rosie Holliday (12)
Killingworth Middle School

LIFE

Life can be difficult in many ways,
You will come across problems,
Which lead you to trouble,
Don't worry alone,
Your friends are there for you.

Life can be difficult in many ways,
There will be some testing times,
Accept them as a challenge,
Some may be tough,
Fun will return.

Life can be difficult in many ways,
Sadness is part of the package,
Don't let it get you down.
If you're broken hearted,
Try to put your troubles behind you,
Let the good times return.

Tina Johnston (12)
Killingworth Middle School

BROTHERLY LOVE

My brother can make me happy or sad,
Sometimes he's evil and makes me go mad.
Most of the time he makes me grin,
Other times he makes an unholy din.
He follows me round and round,
Sneaks up on me without even a sound.
When he's good he's as good as gold,
But when he's bad I wish he could be sold.
Still my brother loves me and I also love him.

James Goodwin (12)
Killingworth Middle School

DANCING ON ICE

Standing tall like a soldier
Making sure everything's in order
Anxious, timid, calm, all in one motion
The shiny white ice looks like creamy lotion
The music begins, soft and light
I start with a split jump and gain great height
I'm timid and tense like a mouse on a bike
The feelings are great as I glide, swoop and skate
My stomach tingles with glee.
I'm excitable, shaky, but I know it's going smoothly
I now try my triple loop as I spin through the air
Then I land on one foot not two, I wouldn't dare
As you skate you feel like a beautiful white swan
Full of pride, full of pace, full of passion and grace.
I end in a spiral then fall to the floor
That is the end of my sequence once more.

Nichola Burns (12)
Killingworth Middle School

HALLOWE'EN

It's Hallowe'en the moon is bright,
Vampires, witches and devils are out
To give us a fright.
Children running around the street
You can hear them singing trick or treat.
People are smelling the supernatural smell
Of the spiritual beings and the mystic paranormal things
Nowadays no one believes in Hallowe'en
Because of science and the logic it brings.

Nicola Collins (12)
Killingworth Middle School

A Fairground Ride - The Water Log

Climbing into the water log
Swerving at the time
Splish, splash on the way
Sitting in a line.

Climbing up to the first drop
Screaming on the way
We're on top of a mountain, a peak
Oh goodness this is the day!

Smile for the camera on the way down
Oh no I'm soaking wet
Now at the bottom of the mountain, the peak
Is it time to go home yet?

Joanne Lord (12)
Killingworth Middle School

I Like Football

I like football in the sun
But in the rain it's still quite fun.
Whenever I am just about to shoot
I give the ball a great big boot.
When I am just about to score
Oh help I hope I don't kick the floor.
Instead of being in goal making a save
I'd rather be in the bath having a bathe.
I support Newcastle United but when they lose
I just feel I've got the blues.
In August the season starts
I'm looking forward to their match against Hearts.

Neil Alan Cook (12)
Killingworth Middle School

THE DREADED TRAFFIC LIGHT

I'm driving along in my motor car,
When the traffic light turns red I haven't got far.

Like a wild animal filled with rage,
With my Aston Martin for a cage.

The traffic light I despise so much,
It makes me stop and break the clutch!

I hate that traffic light with its red blinking eye,
I'll put an end to it and that's not a lie.

I see the traffic light dead ahead
Bang! It's in its eternal bed.

Chris Penfold (13)
Killingworth Middle School

YOUR HEART'S DESIRE

Love burns with desire
You feel like you're on fire
The ache in your heart
Lets you know it's not a lark
If you cherish the boy
You'll know he's not just a toy
If he's passionate
Keep hold of him
Cherish it.
Love is gentle, love is kind,
Love controls your soul and mind.
Love is total, love is caring,
But most of all, love is sharing.

Julie Younger (12)
Killingworth Middle School

AN OUTSTANDING DANCING SHOW

Towering like a giant skyscraper,
The dancer is as light as paper.
Harmonious bells start to chime,
The dancer is perfectly in time.
The first movement is balanced and strong,
I hope she doesn't get one thing wrong.
A one foot poise, she held it well,
The tension was beginning to tell.
The costumes are dazzling and new,
Untidy dancers? Only a few!

Now the next dance, fantastic it's tap,
Heel taps make the sound of a clap.
These dancers are very dedicated,
As a result they're highly rated.
A shuffle ball change a pick up step back,
I couldn't do it, it's rhythm I lack.
The black leotards and silver waistcoats,
Their dancing is in time with the notes.
The crowds are like lions waiting for food,
I do hope the audience aren't too rude.

The next piece of music is for stage,
The dancers are all good for their age.
A very high kick from the back line,
All the costumes are very fine.
Now as the end of the show is near,
It's the grand finale, I feel their fear.
The girls who go first are tall like stilt walkers,
Last the small ones who were told not to be talkers.
Very sadly, it's time to go,
What an outstanding dancing show!

Natasha Barrett (13)
Killingworth Middle School

THUMPER, FOREVER, ALWAYS

Some day in May,
I was given a rabbit.
To give affectionate loving care,
I was happy and glad,
No I was not sad.
Thumper is here to stay, forever, always.

Two years on it still runs away,
It bit my mam, made her mad.
I throw the food away,
'Go away you thankless beast
I hate you, I hate you, so there.'
But Thumper is here to stay, forever, always.

A day later, I couldn't stay mad,
How could I, it's got no sense.
Some days it would go mad and run and run all day,
When I sit upon the step, it comes and snuggles up to me.
Thumper's here to stay forever, always.

Two years on hooray it's my birthday,
At six o'clock I'm out of bed,
I run to mam, same again she sings that song.
'Oh go shut that window it's cold.'
I quickly go to the windowpane,
But stop and stare,
'Oh what's that silly rabbit doing?
Move please, say you're there.'
Clatter, clatter, bang but no,
Thumper's gone, forever, always.

Joanne Lee (13)
Killingworth Middle School

HERE WE GO

Gallop, gallop faster we go
Dodging trees to and fro
Me and this beautiful beast of mine
Always having an outstanding time

Over a hedge, over a gate
No one can catch us at this rate
Up a river, down a bank
We reached the mud and then we sank

First I kicked, then I smacked
First he reared, then he backed
One by one his legs came out
Then he stood up tall, looked about

Off we go the panic is over
The speed we're going we'll reach Dover!

Gallop, gallop faster we go
Dodging trees to and fro.

Danielle Bushbye (12)
Killingworth Middle School

SPACE ALIENS

I woke up in the dead of night
And oh! I got a great big fright
A spaceship that was huge and round
Landed upon our planet's ground

Out stepped a peculiar hideous creature,
Almost as bad as my school teacher!
Green and round with spots all over,
Antennae like a four leaf clover.
Big flat feet, smelly shoes,
Fat long arms, hairy too.

Now it's here what will it do?
It looks as intelligent as a lump of glue!
It moved a step, I looked in its eye
It stared and took a great big sigh.

From which planet could it be,
Saturn, Jupiter, Mercury?
It came to Earth I don't know why,
But know it has to say goodbye!

Rachel Douthwaite (13)
Killingworth Middle School

ALL CREATURES GREAT AND SMALL

There sits the prowler, mean and large
Has a face like a lion, chest like a barge.

She creeps up on her prey,
She tends to do this all day.
They quiver with fear,
But never shed a tear.

The prey are small and frightened,
Sitting in their home their latch is always tightened,
Like my very own home.

They never get a chance to move
They always move when the prowler appears
I know from my experience this is a major fear.

I know it may sound like I own a lion
But for heaven's sake none of them are dying.

So there sits the prowler mean and large
Has a face like a lion, chest like a barge.

Laura Simmister (13)
Killingworth Middle School

WEEKDAYS - SCHOOL

School is somewhere everybody goes,
School is somewhere you have to go.
Teachers will help you when you're stuck,
Friends will help you when you muck up.

We have lessons every day,
Boring, boring, boring!
They can be good but also bad
Anyway we get them five times a day.
Maths, English, science are the lessons
Most days.

On a Friday we all have fun,
We always say 'Only three hours to go'
At 3.30 all you can hear is
'Hip hip hooray it's nearly Saturday.'

Craig J Armstrong (12)
Killingworth Middle School

A VISIT TO THE ARENA

I browsed through the wardrobe to find something to wear,
I was extremely excited, there was magic in the air.
I decided on an outfit and began to get dressed,
Soon I'd be going to the concert, I had to look my best.

We quickly arrived at the arena and we stood to watch the view,
Of crowds bustling and pushing as we waited in the queue.
The men took our tickets and showed us where to go,
We sat and talked for ages then the lights went off for the show.

Shrilling screams surrounded me as the first band entered and sang,
The catchy music was thumping and there was a loud continuous bang.
The atmosphere was sensational, I loved the dancing lights,
As the concert kept on going, all through the night.

The show was over quickly, I thought it was far too soon,
As we drove home very happy by the light of the sparkling moon.
I got home and put on my pyjamas then brushed my teeth and hair,
And I waited in anticipation for the show again next year.

Alison Walker (12)
Killingworth Middle School

WHAT A LITTLE MONSTER!

I open up the door to see a little face,
Sitting in mud and chewing up my shoelace.
I look in amazement at what I can see,
She reaches out her arms and looks up to me.

I've cleaned up the carpet, sat her in the chair,
But dare I attempt to brush that tatty curly hair?
I take out the brush and slip it into my pocket,
As I do her eyes jump out of their sockets.
She runs and runs and will not stop,
Until I pull out a lollipop.

Soon she sits with me calm and snug,
I turn and give her a delicious caring hug.
I know she's sometimes a little pain,
But I know I love her all the same.

Stacey Hogg (12)
Killingworth Middle School

PSYCHO WAYNE

I know a cat named Psycho Wayne,
He's completely bonkers and insane.

He rustles into people's vile rotten bins,
To look for food like fish's fins.

Psycho Wayne tries to gnaw people's slippers,
As well as fish's fins, he adores fresh kippers.

Old Psycho's not afraid to get into a fight,
This ragged feline used to be white.

Now he's dirty and covered in muck,
He got knocked down by an oncoming truck.

He is a good cat or should I say used to be,
Rest in peace - RIP.

Andrew Hunter (12)
Killingworth Middle School

FRIENDS AND ENEMIES

A friend is someone you can trust,
A friend is someone who can help you,
By helping you in a bad situation.
He is your ally, mate, pal, companion.

An enemy is a person who you can't trust,
An enemy is a person who will not help you,
By failing to help you in a bad situation,
He is your foe, competitor, opponent.

Scott Carruthers (12)
Killingworth Middle School

FRIENDSHIP

A friend will always be there for you,
No matter what you say or do.
In good times and bad they're always there,
To lend a hand and show they care.
They cheer you up when you feel blue,
And this is what a friend should do.

Being willing to confide,
And see the other person's side,
Showing trust and care each day,
Living in a loving way.

I hope I can be all these things,
I'll wait and see what friendship brings.

Andrew McKale (12)
Killingworth Middle School

MY REFLECTION

Every day when I wake up
I have a good look
To see if it's still there
Oh my God. look at my hair

Every day and every night
He's still there in my sight
Everything I do
He does too!

I smashed the mirror
Then suddenly, there wasn't one
There was none!

Marc Thompson (12)
Longbenton Community College

ALL THE WORLD'S A . . .

All the world's a netball court,
All the women and girls merely players.
They have their exits and their entrances,
One woman in her time shoots many nets,
Her matches being eight different shots,
First the toddler practising by crawling with the ball in one hand
Up to a toy box and dropping it in,
Then the infant in the nursery standing about a metre away
From a bucket and throwing a ball to see if it would go in,
Then the little girl starting to practise her shoulder passes,
Bounce passes, chest passes and her overhead throws
With the coach,
Then the junior practising her dodging and shooting on the court,
Then the teenager shooting many nets and scoring in her
First match of the season,
Then the sixth former playing for the county
Trying her best to score against the opposition,
Then the professional playing for England
Dodging, shooting, passing and scoring,
Then the elderly lady talking to her grandchildren about
What it was like being a professional netball player.

Danielle McMeekin (13)
Longbenton Community College

THE BIG MATCH

Home team enters the stadium,
Crowd gives a roar,
Sounding like a pride of lions
Gathering for a kill.

Rain evacuates the clouds,
Looking like miniature men
Parachuting from an aeroplane,
Covering the short green turf.

Rasping whistle of the referee
Signals the start of the match.
Drums pound to a chorus of singing,
Echoing around the ground.

An ocean of coloured shirts
Dominate the ground,
A mass of hats and scarves are thrown
When a goal is scored.

Aidan Bell (12)
Longbenton Community College

ALL THE WORLD'S A . . .

All the world's an airport,
And all the men and women are merely planes;
They have their arrivals and departures;
And one man in his time flies many routes,
His flights being seven ages. At first the glider,
Diving and swooping like a bird in the arms of the wind;
Then the propeller aircraft, slowly creeping to its destination
Like a snail,
And then the Concorde swiftly, lovingly swimming through the air.
Then a prototype jet trying desperately to prove itself
Even when faced with rejection.
Then the jumbo jet, at its peak doing its daily routine;
And so he plays his part.
The sixth age shifts into the ageing World War II fighter,
With wings and controls rusting and out of date,
With its youthful engine drone.
Last scene of all, that ends in this strange, eventful flight,
Is second childishness; and mere oblivion,
Sans wings, sans, engine, sans cockpit, sans everything.

Robbie Walker (13)
Longbenton Community College

ALL THE WORLD'S A BOOK

All the world's a book,
And all the men and women are merely actors of my imagination,
They have their openings and their conclusions,
And one book in its time has many parts,
His act being seven chapters,
At first the introduction explaining and exploring
The start of the book,
Then the first chapter anticipating what's going to happen
In the second one,
Second one has come now knowing what has happened,
But the third still awaits,
Getting older now as you read more and more,
Your knowledge is extending,
Chapter four, the longest, life dragging on your back,
Little excitement left,
The fifth, disappointment of what has turned out to be,
The sixth chapter, long and hard
Never thought this would be,
Last chapter of all, you read the last few pages of your book,
Like the last few days of your life,
As you close the book you close your eyes,
Never to live or read again,
Rest forever.

Stephanie Bell (13)
Longbenton Community College

ALL THE WORLD'S A . . .

All the world's a drum kit,
And all the men and women are merely drums;
They have their beats and their rests;
And one man in his time plays many rhythms,
His movements being seven ages.
At first the tambourine,
Its cymbals clashing and the cheap plastic skin,
Annoying his parents.
Then the tom-tom drum attached to the main kit,
Banging out the high pitched sound,
Practising his Grade One piece,
And then the conga,
Playing a soothing rhythm hypnotising his loved ones.
Then the snare drum, rolling out the marching beat
At a steady pace,
And then the bass, big, bold and proud
Bashing his simple rhythm
Ruling out everything else.
Last of all the actual kit
Playing his old favourite rock beat
With slow and boring variations to end this wonderful piece.
Crash.

Christopher Hall (13)
Longbenton Community College

ALL THE WORLD'S A . . .

All the world's a dream,
And all the men and women merely
figures of your imagination,
One person in this dream goes through many stages,
Their stages being seven ages. Firstly when you get into the bed
the cold hits you, a slap, suddenly you have warmth.
Secondly when you first fall asleep but you know you're sleeping
so you control the dream. And then the sleep when everything
gets light and bubbly, and you feel like you're floating. Then
the deep sleep, when everything is intense and you won't wake
for anything. And then the nightmare with its scary
monsters that run after you. The sixth stage is the hero, who
fights away the monster and carries you into the sunset.
The last stage, you awake, there are no more
Snuggling and no more happy endings . . .
Just life.

Stacey King (13)
Longbenton Community College

ALL THE WORLD'S A GREENHOUSE

All the world's a Greenhouse
And all the plants and flowers merely people
Seedlings start to grow like a baby not yet born
Roots and shoots peek through the soil like arms
And legs moving
As they are fed they grow big and strong like sturdy children
And soon they become adults like flowers
Blossoming in a garden
But time goes by and petals start to fall
And flowers and people wither and die.

Richard Caisley (14)
Longbenton Community College

ALL THE WORLD'S AN ORCHESTRA . . .

All the world's an orchestra
And all the men and women are merely notes on a stave,
They have their introductions and their finales,
And one man in his time plays many parts
His acts being seven performances.

At first the practice
Screeching and squeaking at the conductor's directions;
Then the introduction, with violins and cellos slowly ascending
A chromatic scale.
And then the waltz,
A woodwind duet
With romantic melodies and harmonies
Which cause the audience to flood.
Then a march,
In strange rhythms played by polished tubas, proud trumpeters,
Sudden and dramatic with dynamics, constantly accelerating
Even after the conductor's glares.
And then the pianist's solo
In thick textures with echoing dynamics
With perfect notes and precise fingerings,
Full of complicated rhythms and unusual melodies.
The sixth piece moves key into C major,
The orchestral performance,
Starting with loud bass but ending in the treble clef with
                                        oboes and flutes.
Last bars of all that end this strange and dramatic performance is
repetition; Sans strings, sans woodwind, sans brass, sans audience.

Gemma Brewis (13)
Longbenton Community College

ALL THE WORLD IS A BOOK

All the world is a book,
And all the men and women are merely characters,
They have their exits and their entrances,
And one character in their time plays many parts,
Their acts being seven chapters. Chapter one, the newly
Born baby, changing the lives of two people.
Next, chapter two, the infant, at work, at rest and at play,
Leading a normal happy life.
Next chapter three, the college graduate, black robe with
Hat and tassel. Next, chapter four, the married, responsible
Adult, responsible job and life.
Next, chapter five, the retired, lonely widow, remarried but
Life not the same. Next, chapter six, coming very near
To the end of her time, with nothing to look
Forward to, until the end. Last chapter of all,
That ends this sad eventful novel,
Is another lonely, sad book, as this woman
Loses everything.

Alex Weatherstone (13)
Longbenton Community College

MY FAIRY LAND

Beyond, beyond the horizon line,
The mountains and the plains,
That crown the western border,
There lies that fairy land of mine.
Unseen to all but the eyes of the beholder.

The grass is green, like emeralds rare,
Its waters clear like my window of dreams.
The fairy castles hang in the air,
And purple trees in masses
And noble knights and ladies fair
Come riding down the green grasses.

To me, they say if I could stand
Upon the mountain ledges
I should but see on either hand
Bland fields and dusty hedges
And yet I know my fairy land
Lies somewhere deep inside my heart.

Nikita Lye (12)
Longbenton Community College

ALL THE WORLD'S A FOOTBALL TEAM

All the world's a football team,
And the men merely players;
They have their kick-offs and their full times;
And one player in his time plays many matches,
His career being seven ages. At first the schoolboy, playing
In make-believe Wembley for the glory of the cup;
Then the high-spirited youngster, using his speed and
Agility to his advantage. Fighting for a first team place;
Then the pro, he got his place and now he's using his
Dazzling skill and goal scoring technique to impress even
The top class teams.
Now the England superstar, who's name is on everybody's lips:
Now he's old and forgotten
An unused reserve, its time to hang up his boots.
And then the manager, with wise words and sound advice
From his experiences;
Last scene of all,
That ends the era of this eventful history,
Is the legend, although he's gone he'll always be
Remembered and never forgotten.

Gavin Dodds (13)
Longbenton Community College

THE GLORY DAYS

It was a mild October afternoon
Oh what a fateful day
We weren't really very hopeful
When Man United came to play

We'd been hammered down at Wembley
In the Charity Shield
But that was soon forgotten
As Newcastle took the field

Newcastle started brightly
The Geordies were impressed
Then Shearer leapt as if on springs
And Peacock did the rest

The linesman signalled for a goal
The judgement was proved right
But Schmeichel wasn't happy
And his nose shone like a light

The Red Devils were unsettled
But we weren't finished yet
Ginola turned Neville inside out
And nearly burst the net.

The Man U team weren't happy
As the half-time whistle sounded
Cantona showed his big lip
As on the ref he rounded.

The second half was started
And the Geordies danced with glee
When Shearer crossed into the box
And Les notched number three.

But it still wasn't over
And you should have heard the din
When Schmeichel made two canny saves
Before Shearer knocked it in

The Geordies were on fire
And poured forward yet again
The Man U were streaming out
As Prince Albert lobbed the Dane

And when the final whistle blew
The job was now complete
We hit the town
And began dancing in the street.

Dean Crossland (12)
Longbenton Community College

THE PLANT

The bulldozers dug to the ground
Turning round and round

The bulldozers suddenly stopped at a crash.
The men stared at it, something large.

'What is that' said a girl.
'It's a giant plant from years ago when they lived on the planet,'

It is the last of its kind.
The plant was as tall as ten men.

It was as brown as an oak fireplace with
Green leaves like a flower's petals.

It was a tree.

Mark Tait (12)
Longbenton Community College

BONFIRE NIGHT

On the 5th of November night starts to set in
The sky is red like a bright fiery flame
It is becoming darker every moment of the day

It is now seven o'clock and the fire is being lit
Now it's pitch black
The fire spits up into the sky.
It crackles, hisses and spits
Fireworks stand in a row, ready to be lit
Then suddenly
Whoosh, whoosh, whoosh
They are shot up in the air
And a shower of colours falls gently to the ground,
Up they go again and again and fall.

Now the fire's burnt out
The fireworks are gone
Everyone's gone home
The night lies still
And on the 6th of November, day starts to set in.

Rachel Goodfellow (12)
Longbenton Community College

SEASONS

The nights are light
The days are bright
The bulbs start growing
And the birds start singing
What is it?

The nights are long,
The days are warm
The sun shines bright
And you can hear the sound of children.
What is it?

The nights are dark
The wind is cold
The leaves change colour
And drop to the ground.
What is it?

The nights are long
The days are short
The weather is cold
And we try to get warm.
What is it?

James Spence (13)
Longbenton Community College

ALL THE WORLD'S A FOOTBALL MATCH

All the world's a football match,
And all the men and women merely players;
They have their exits and their entrances;
And one man in his career scoring many goals,
His career being seven stages. At first the toddler dribbling
The ball in the back lane.
Then the ambitious school boy dreaming of playing at Wembley.
Then the willing reserve trying desperately to make it into
The first team and make a good impression,
The fourth age shifts into the regular first team player and
Captain, and a place in the England team; his future's good.
Then the player coming into his retirement years, tired
Limbs and ageing mind force him to hang up his boots.
Now into the sixth age the experimenting manager, hoping
To get a championship team together.
Then the final stage the housebound, crippled person with
The blurred vision and the weakening ears. This football
Legend comes to the end of his triumphant life.

Chris Aldridge (14)
Longbenton Community College

ALL THE WORLD'S A FOOTBALL MATCH

All the world's a football match,
And all the people are merely players;
They have their good matches and their bad ones;
And one person in her time plays many matches,
At first a little child
Just running about kicking the ball in any direction.
Then the girl getting better
Begging for some football boots.
Then the teenager with her private coach
Aiming to be a professional with the skills she's got.
The fourth stage is her big day
She's on the field waiting for the whistle to blow
All her supporters watching and shouting
This is her biggest match yet.
She's much older than she was
Exhausted as the half time whistle went.
But when the final whistle goes,
She knows this was her last and final best match.
Last scene of all she resigns and starts coaching as a
Manager,
Hoping still to be famous and teach the skill she's been taught,
To the young ones aiming to go all the way to the top.

Rose Boldon (14)
Longbenton Community College

CHRISTMAS

It's Christmas, dad
The sun's appearing over the horizon
Just like thirteen years ago

It's Christmas, dad,
Big presents and trees appear in my head
Just like thirteen years ago

It's Christmas, dad
Our yard is covered with snow, looking like a snowland
Just like thirteen years ago

It's Christmas, dad
I want to be with you
Just like thirteen years ago

Joong Bae (13)
Longbenton Community College

THE ALIENS ARE OUT THERE!

Aliens they're funny things,
Giant heads and flapping wings.
Flying about in their UFO,
People to see and places to go.
Another Mars Attacks it could be.
People running and start to flee.
But then again they could be nice,
Living on a planet made of snow and ice.
They could have a weird little language all of their own
And even Jupiter could be their home.
Zapping machines and a laser gun
Might provide the aliens with hours of fun.
So when you look up and see a twinkling light,
You'll jump with joy or run in fright!
So now to the reader of this poem,
When it's late and you're wandering home,
The aliens may be looking down on you
While having tea with Dr Who!

Cara Middlemass (12)
Longbenton Community College

THE RACE

On your marks
Get set
Go!

You're out of the blocks
Stride for stride
With everyone else

Your arms are going as fast as lightning
Your legs are going as fast as an express train
Your eyes are fixed on the finish

Across the line
Click!
The stopwatch stopped

Your time 9.98 seconds

Sarah Hunter (13)
Longbenton Community College

THE DRAGON

The scaly beast with silver scales, teeth like knives and barbed-end tail.
The serpent beast moving like a snake. Wings raised high it takes
$\qquad\qquad\qquad\qquad\qquad\qquad$ to the sky.
The horned beast, razor claws, gnarled horns and armoured skin
$\qquad\qquad\qquad\qquad\qquad\qquad$ as hard as steel.
The winged beast with wings like leather, scorching breath on
$\qquad\qquad\qquad\qquad\qquad\qquad$ the heather.
The dragon, the dragon, breath as hot as the sun.
The dragon, the dragon, unto you your death is done.

Jake Wilson Craw (12)
Longbenton Community College

When I Grow Up

When I grow up I want to be
A footballer who's on TV
I want to be famous, I want to be rich
I want to play on that football pitch.

I'll get the ball over the line
My shirt number will be number nine
I'll be top scorer after every game
Everyone will know my name.

I never get tackled
I never miss
The crowd will cheer
They wouldn't hiss.

A little turn here
A little turn there
Defenders look out
Keepers beware.

My teachers say I can't
My parents say 'No'
I'm better than Shearer
Even Ronaldo

In my dreams
I make a vow
I'll be a footballer
Ten years from now.

I know I can make it
I'll go all the way
I'll get to be a footballer
Some day, some day . . .

Tom Surtees (12)
Longbenton Community College

EMOTIONS

A smile
The sun comes out
A tear
The rain pours down
Anger
Lightning strikes again
Thunder
Caused by a frown
Bad mood
A storm is brewing
Good thoughts
The sun shines on
Envy
Night arrives once more
Darkness
All light has gone

Katie Symes (13)
Longbenton Community College

SPACE

Five, four, three, two, one *Blast off*
We're flying to the moon
We are going so fast
We will get there soon

Zooming through the clouds
Into the bright, yellow sun
It is getting hot now
But the fun has just begun

We are miles away from Earth
And I am feeling homesick
I look down to Earth and what do I see
My country and home in Perth

We are landing on the moon
In the black lonely spaces
We put on our suits and took our first step
But our steps were more like great big paces

Five, four, three, two, one *Blast off*
We're flying back to Earth
We are getting very close now
I can see my town in Perth

Angela Connolly (12)
Longbenton Community College

ALL THE WORLD'S A FOOTBALL PITCH

All the world's a football pitch
And all the men are merely players
They have their kick-offs, half-times and full-times.
His game being seven seasons
At first the junior breaking into the first team
Scoring goals for fun in the reserves
Then the boy with his new boots.
Jogging happily on to the pitch
And then the defender, staring into the eyes of the opposition.
Making hard tackles
Then the midfielder, full of running, tackling and shooting
And the captain, the leader and proud of it
Seeking a place in the England team
Then the centre forward
Scoring goals, goals and more goals
With golden boots he is now the elite
Now the last season as he lifts the world cup
To a perfect game.

Chris Chaffey (13)
Longbenton Community College

FRIENDS

Friends, friends, friends
Should be there in the bad times
With you in the good times
Helping you with your problems
Friends are not about being
Pretty or ugly, fat or thin
Tall, short, clever or not
It's their personality, their attitude, their feelings
That count.
Friends are friends if they respect you
If they stick up for you
If they trust you
If they tell you the truth
If they like you for who you are.

Suzanne McGregor (12)
Longbenton Community College

THE STARS

The stars twinkled in the sky,
Like the sugar on a pie,
They are like a diamond up above
They twinkle like a colourful dove.

The stars twinkled in the sky,
Like the sugar on a pie,
Wishing, shooting, north and south,
You are so amazed you open your mouth.

The stars twinkled in the sky,
Like the sugar on a pie,
Little dots in the dark
they twinkle on a tree's bark.

The stars twinkled in the sky,
Like the sugar on a pie,
The sky is so black
It's like being in a sack.

The stars twinkled in the sky
Like the sugar on a pie,
They twinkle like a happy baby's eye,
The stars in the sky.

Rebecca Edwards (13)
Longbenton Community College

ALL THE WORLD'S A WEATHER MAP . . .

All the world's a weather map,
And all the men and women are merely weather systems,
They have their fronts and ridges,
And one man in his time plays many weather types,
Their act being several seasons. Firstly the rainbow
Beaming with light;
Secondly the heavens open to a young girl being
Dragged to school, sighing and crying,
Third the sunshine symbolising the happiness of a first love.
Forth the thunder and lightning as the anguish of the
Shotgun shoots the soldier to the ground.
Fifth the white clouds settle as a smart dressed man
Is cleared from the court, with a sigh of relief.
Sixth the grey clouds make an entrance as an old man
Sits with his paper in one hand, and a mug of soup in another
Sighing and waiting to see what's around the next corner;
And finally the world comes to a painful, slow end
As the hail stones smash viciously off a slate roof
Gradually tearing it apart.
Sans, sun, sans rain, sans hail, sans everything.

Amy Ferguson (14)
Longbenton Community College

YOU'RE DIFFERENT

You're different from me
Or am I different from you?
Your eyes are dark brown,
Yet mine are light blue.
Your skin is quite dark,
And mine is quite light
is there any real difference?
Am I wrong?
Are you right?
You wear bright dresses
I wear sports clothes,
I wear studs in my ears,
You wear yours in your nose.
My skin is unmarked,
While yours is tattooed.
I eat only vegetables
You live on junk food.
I am a Christian
You're a Hindu
My friend's a Muslim
Your friend's a Jew
I throw away millions,
You beg for a pound
I live in a mansion,
You sleep on the ground.
My eyesight is perfect
While yours is so weak,
You wear thick glasses
But I look the geek.
I go to the gym,
People love my physique,
But you couch potato,
watch the telly all week.

My hair is jet black
Yours is silvery grey,
I shouldn't speak too soon
Mine'll be the same some day.

What it boils down to
is simple to see.
I'm equal to you
And you're equal to me.

Stephanie Barlow (12)
Longbenton Community College

ALL THE WORLD'S A ZOO

All the world's a zoo,
And all the people merely animals,
One person in their lifetime is many animals,
Their life being in seven stages,
At first the baby koala lying softly in the mother's arms,
Then the naughty monkey sneaking around and
Stealing other monkeys' possessions,
And then the love birds never leaving each other's
Sight, not bearing to be separated,
Then the elephants staying together while the
Lionesses attack, keeping each other safe,
And then the graceful dressage horse never making a
Mistake, each foot placed neatly down, turning
Gracefully,
The sixth age is a camel, old and brittle, wandering the
Plains alone,
The last animal is the rhino, old, tired and his
Leathered skin cracked, dreaming of his days gone by.

Zoë Bowlt (13)
Longbenton Community College

ALL THE WORLD'S A CAKE

All the world's a cake,
And all the men and women merely tasters,
They have their sponges and their creams,
And one cake alone has many layers,
The cake having seven layers.

At first the tiny butterfly cake with a simple sponge and cream.

Then the gingerbread man,
With his smarties and his glowing jelly nose,
He's still like a stone, never moving.

And then the chocolate chip cookie made tasty in the oven,
With lots of chocolate chips and the chocolate mixture
Surrounding the chips.

Then a Victoria sponge, full of thick strawberry jam,
With a rich vanilla sponge all golden,
A mouth-watering prospect,
Seeking to be eaten by a nice, quiet boy,
Not by a bubbly character.

And then the joyful time of Christmas cake,
With sweet, white icing,
And nice piped decoration,
With white little fat snowmen on.

The penultimate stage of all is the 5 tiers,
All being different from the one below,
The one below being bigger,
And at the top two marzipan people,
A bride and a groom.

Last cake of all a wimpy little fairy cake,
Which ends this cake's life,
In a few seconds mere crumbs,
Sans icing, sans sponge, sans marzipan, sans everything.

Ian Pratt (13)
Longbenton Community College

ALL THE WORLD'S A FAIRY TALE BOOK

All the world's a fairy tale book,
And all the men and women merely characters,
They have their introduction and their conclusions,
And one character in his time plays many parts,
His acts being several chapters,

First of all birth, a baby is born,
Placed in a bassinet, and sleeping soundly,
And then the schoolboy, off to school to learn,
Then the teenager, looking for trouble,
And adventure and usually finding it,

Then the prince, fighting the dragons, and
Wanting the princess's hand in marriage,
The proud king next, full of old tales of mystical,
Times and fighting dragons,
Then the sixth stage, where he must make way,
For a new king, he is too old to carry on,
And everyone wants a younger king,

This is the end, he is too old,
He dies.

Jemma Gallagher (14)
Longbenton Community College

FALLING OVER

I've just fallen over,
and it really hurt too,
Every time I put my foot down,
It hu . . . *Oooohhh!*

I've just fallen over,
And it was on the ice,
I went *slip! Kerplonk!*
It wasn't very nice.

I've just fallen over,
And I cut my arm,
Uh-oh! It's bleeding again!
Remember - keep calm!

I've just fallen over
And I hurt my ankle
I'll have to have a look,
It wasn't my leg - thankful!

I've just fallen over
And I'm hurting all over - *Ow!*
Ok, ok,
I'll stop whining now!

Kayleigh Dunn (12)
Longbenton Community College

ALL THE WORLD'S A CRYING SESSION

All the world's a crying session
And all the men and women merely victims;
They have their joyful and traumatising tears
And one man in his lifetime sheds many tears,
His tears being for seven causes, at first the FA Cup Final,
Players joyfully shed their tears on national TV;
Then the crying schoolboy, with his tissue and
Distressed face, strolling unwillingly to school
And then romantic tears dripping on the lady's hand as he
Proposes very confidently. Then the angry tear full of honour,
Which boxing brilliantly demonstrates as
The fighters clench their fist for their country
And then the admittance tear which may appear in court of law
Quite often, as the victim is so guilty of the crime.
The sixth tear is for making up, as the wife finally
Ends the seven months of absentness from her husband
For the guilty affair that couldn't have been helped or could it?
As that is where the sorrow tear comes in for the family
That has just lost their son, the most truthful one,
Mere death, sans teeth, sans eyes, sans taste, sans everything.

Robert Jobson (13)
Longbenton Community College

CLEAR DIAMONDS

Pure mist and moist air was flooding around my vision,
it was a smell of a damp, wet day,
the raindrops were sliding down the window
the splashing drops gave me a fright as they hit the fresh rainbow,
the taste was cold and wet
but I still wanted to stay in my vision of clear diamonds.

Anna Anderson (12)
Sacred Heart Comprehensive School

WATERCOLOURS

Unaware of goings on around me,
the relaxation begins
colours, thoughts and dreams swirling up around me.
A blank space to fill with thoughts and theories
with a distinct lack of surroundings,
beginning to think,
I see new things,
things I never knew before enter my mind,
half of which drain as I try to remember
I put what thoughts I have to paper,
pick up an HB pencil
and begin to scribble
tree shapes, long and fluffy at the top with
the saddened greenish leaves.
I draw . . .
puddles, dark and murky
yet only millimetres deep
grey lines marking a rectangle shape with windows
with a warm red brick design.
Two horses prancing only newly broken in,
only one noise could be heard,
the rain (just a slight drizzle) tapping,
tapping on the thick window panes.
The smell of the humid air absorbed by the landscape
I begin to paint now,
the sky is a blue topaz watercolour
spotted with pearl stars,
emerald painted meadows . . .
and it's done.

The masterpiece is completed!

Charlie Stephenson (13)
Sacred Heart Comprehensive School

MY PLACE

I watch the slow stream of water going into the small lake
It flows free like a pet being let out of its cage
Then everything is peaceful.

The stone is so smooth so when I sit down I can hardly feel my bum
As I stare at the hills from my stone, I can see letters forming.
They are jumping out at me wanting to be made into words,
But if I give them that attention, I would spend all day doing that.
I don't want to.

A tent peg is sticking half way out of the ground.
The top is oddly shaped and rusty.
I know someone hasn't been here for a long time.

I wish I could take a photo of everything,
But I don't think the land would like it.
It wants to be left untouched, unharmed from pollution and rubbish.
It wants to be free.

Catherine Quinn (12)
Sacred Heart Comprehensive School

A FALLING SENSATION

It drips and drops,
It pitters and patters,
It glistens and glitters,
It chases itself down the smooth glass window,
It falls and falls horizontally but slowly,
Then gently rests itself in the most wonderful manner,
On the green paradise beneath itself.

Natalie Chapman (12)
Sacred Heart Comprehensive School

SECRETS OF A FOREST

I tiptoed on, my heart in my mouth,
I can hear a drip, drop of the raindrops leaping from one leaf to another.
For as far as I can see there is nothing but thick, deep forest.
Each branch of the tall trees has lots of little rainbows
                               drooping off the end.
Green, red, yellow and brown splashed upon them.
I can hear a deep sound
'Tu-whit tu-whoo, tu-whit tu-whoo'
It's an owl, it must be getting late.
It starts to rain again.
Before I know it I'm surrounded by water.
I dash off as fast as my legs will carry me.
I reach an open space where I camp for the night.
Hopefully the day will be brighter tomorrow.

Emma Lumsden (12)
Sacred Heart Comprehensive School

SENSATION

As I walk through the forest,
I see three colours standing out at me,
Red, brown and green.
All these colours give me a warm
Sensation, right through.
When I get the sensation,
It feels rather like when you
Have a nice cup of milky coffee,
On a cold winter's day.

Gemma Cairns (12)
Sacred Heart Comprehensive School

AUTUMN IS HERE

I look out of my window,
I see the sky as white as snow,
The leaves that were once a fresh and healthy green
Are now a rusty orange.
The droopy wet flowers glisten in the light of the golden sun.
The dew on the petals shine.
The insects scuttle among the tall grass.
The branches on the trees sway gently like
Octopus in the wind.
The leaves rustle.

Autumn is here.

Lyndsey Howarth (12)
Sacred Heart Comprehensive School

HOLIDAYS

Clear skies, white sand,
Hot sun, blue sea
I'm going abroad this year
I can't wait, I'll get away from my parents
But I'll miss all of my friends
I can't wait, I can't wait
Grey skies, black paths,
Cold rain, endless fog
I didn't go on holiday this year
I didn't get away from my parents
I'm desperate to see my friends
I can't wait for school, I can't wait for school.

Julie Davidson (12)
Sacred Heart Comprehensive School

THE NIGHT WHISPERS

The diamonds are hanging in the sky
A young girl hears something
'Night is coming. Night is coming.'
She's young, so young and all alone.
She hears whispers of wondering words,
Running, wanting, waiting
She starts to run with the words
'Run from night, run from night.'
A velvet, dark scarf falls onto the diamonds.
She runs towards . . . The Night Whispers
In a clearing in a forest she hears whispers of curiosity.
Wisps of coldness spin around her
Spinning, spinning, spinning.
She can't get away from the voices
Laughing, screaming, watching
The girl hears a piercing scream and screams herself
Was she a Night Whisper now?

Michelle Jackson (12)
Sacred Heart Comprehensive School

MOONLIGHT MAGIC

A thin silver delicate moon shines down on a frozen lake
Nothing moves, everything is still, the world has come to a halt.
Then a single blue diamond falls from the sky and silently fades away
And just as I think it is gone forever
A white wave slithers across the icy surface of the lake.
More and more follow, getting smaller and smaller
Until the lake is still again.
Slowly the silent moon slides behind a silver edged cloud.
Dawn breaks, the world awakens.
But the magic secretly sleeps.

Frances Marshall (12)
Sacred Heart Comprehensive School

A WALK ALONG THE BEACH

Splish, splash, splish, splash
As the tall, wet tropical trees
Blow with the gentle breeze of the waves,
The spray of the ocean
Continues to blow up to the shore.

Splish, splash, splish, splash
As I walk along the shore the sand is soft as snow
And my feet sink into the sand.
They go further and further under
Until you can't see them anymore.

Splish, splash, splish, splash.

Lisa Howey (12)
Sacred Heart Comprehensive School

RAIN

I sit alone and wonder why,
the drops of water fall from the sky,
why it's cold and wet and there's no light,
why the drops are such a sight.

The feel of rain treading your face,
I sit and think and fall in a daze,
I feel so fresh, alive and well,
as the drops of crystals quickly fell.

The muddy grass, the sky so deep,
the water drips from leaf to leaf,
the dullness outside, the thought in my head,
it's bright in my house but it feels so dead.

Stacey Smith (12)
Sacred Heart Comprehensive School

DARK, DREARY DAY

It is a dark, dreary day,
Nobody in sight,
Everybody is inside because of this dull light.

Raindrops dripping off the rooftops,
Water drips from leaf to leaf
All the leaves are full of water.
It is freezing cold.

There is a tree trunk that has split in half,
As the water trickles down.
The grass is soaked through,
The rain will not stop.
The gutters are full of water as the rain comes down.

Rebecca Mohan (12)
Sacred Heart Comprehensive School

RAIN

Drip drop of water
splashing onto the long green fingers
of the leaves,
dropping, dropping
to the ground making the most wonderful sound.
It trickles gently to a drain in the corner of the
playground.
As it *slithers* to the *drain*
it falls and splashes
with a loud plopping.

Toni Kennedy (12)
Sacred Heart Comprehensive School

TRAPPED

Life just feels meaningless,
you feel like you're living with hell.
All alone in such a big world,
you feel so low it's so
dull and dark, you're
>Trapped
You have a terrible fear inside
of you, it all goes cold, you feel
like death, you shout help,
Your voice just echoes as if
you're standing in an empty
corridor, nobody can hear you,
you're suddenly
>Trapped
You try to bottle it all up
inside but it's no good, you go
mad, let everything out, scream,
you're
>Trapped.

Carly Willumsen (13)
Sacred Heart Comprehensive School

WEATHER

The mist is clear throughout the sky,
the sun is out,
the wind is blowing,
the lake is crystal clear.
Autumn is coming around again,
the trees are bare,
the leaves are brown,
as the rain starts falling down.

Helen Bell (12)
Sacred Heart Comprehensive School

DEEP, DEEP, DREAMING

I was looking out of my steamed window,
As it started to rain.
Nothing but greyness above me,
Nothing but greenness below me.
Droopy leaves on the trees,
Raindrops bouncing off them.
The sweet smell of dampness all around,
Scared worms peeping through the ground.
Clashing and bashing on the window,
It sounds like the beating of drums.
Animals scurrying through the moist grass,
Rustling and weaving through each strand.
I felt all cosy and warm,
On this cold, wet winter's day.
All I could do was stare,
As nature passed me by.

Susanne Wardley (12)
Sacred Heart Comprehensive School

TRAPPED IN DARKNESS

Life can be full of emptiness,
When you are feeling so alone,
No one to turn to,
Just a passage which you are trapped in.

Misery is taking over your life,
And a big part inside of you is missing.
Depression blackens your mind,
And loneliness is overwhelming inside.

For pain is the road to happiness.

Leanne Kaprelian (13)
Sacred Heart Comprehensive School

IMAGINATION

Alone in the house,
not even the squeak of a mouse.
Now's the chance.
You feel unhappy, torn,
you start shouting for help,
but nobody's there.
You can't stop yourself,
you hear people shouting -
I hate you, I hate you, I hate you!
The pills are there in front of you,
you're saying no,
but you think of all the disasters you've caused,
all the stress in school,
how much you think people hate you,
you grab the pill box,
put your hand out
and take two pills to soothe that thumping headache.

Roisin O'Donnell (13)
Sacred Heart Comprehensive School

RAIN

While sitting on the fresh green grass,
Watching the golden leaves blow past,
I sat for a while thinking why all those flowers had to die.
In the distance the crystal clear river was flowing by,
Above was the golden sunshine in the sky,
All of a sudden a black cloud came,
Oh no! Not the rain.

Victoria Parry (12)
Sacred Heart Comprehensive School

MYSTICAL PLACE

I am sitting in a classroom and it's a dull, dark day
but while the teacher's talking
I'm somewhere else
I'm in a place with fresh green grass and
tall trees that have high golden leaves.
I'm with high mountains which
are covered in creamy white snow.
I'm in a place with bright blue butterflies
and scarlet red ladybirds.
I'm lying in this daydream and it disappears
I look outside the dripping rain falling from leaf to leaf
the raindrops racing down the windows.
I'm back in that classroom with the same teacher talking
and I can't go back to that mystical place.

Jade Adams (12)
Sacred Heart Comprehensive School

EMPTINESS . . .

Emptiness is when I'm laying in my bed,
the darkness hanging over me,
strangling me,
covering me in sadness,
making me feel isolated,
the desperation of wanting -
needing to get out,
of where?
Me?
The depths of my misery,
I'm trapped, empty.

Helen Chapman (13)
Sacred Heart Comprehensive School

THE BEACH

I walk up the slippery dunes with my towel.
I'm going to my favourite place.
I put down my things and take off those sandy flip-flops.
Suddenly I get a whoosh of salty sea air.
A crab walks promptly past me,
Is that a falling star stranded on the shore?
Oh no, it's only a starfish waving its arms around.

I stride through the rock pools, 'splish splosh'.
Yuck, I can feel all that slimy seaweed crawling in my toes,
The rocks feel like daggers in my feet but do not bleed.

It's getting dark now, and I've been having so much fun
That I didn't realise the time.
That lovely burnt amber sun is setting in the distance,
Now I have to go home into my lovely cosy bed.

Samantha Gourley (12)
Sacred Heart Comprehensive School

LONELINESS

I listen to the sound of the rain falling down my window,
prayin' for a gentle wind to bring my baby back again.
Trying to be strong, but I'm not getting any stronger.
I'm feeling all alone and unwanted inside.
The depression is tight, and there's no escape to the way I feel.
Loneliness, it's tearing away this heart of mine.
I lie awake 'cause I can't take another night.
Lonely, it's been too long, I can't hold on any more.

Deborah Wilkinson (13)
Sacred Heart Comprehensive School

FEELINGS

Illness,
       can lead to
Death,
       will lead to
Misery,
       is heading into
Darkness,
       may be leading to
Despair,
       is heading into
Emptiness,
       is making you feel
Trapped,
       you're now in
Desperation,
       which is turning to
Depression,
       you're feeling drowsy . . .
       Drowsy . . . black!
You're missing someone and you're alone?
You're cold, and you're helpless!

Sharon Baird (13)
Sacred Heart Comprehensive School

TEARDROPS

I can't bear them.
Tears.
Tears burn my face.
Laughter incinerates my tears,
but laughter is hard.
Too hard.
Not the way I am feeling.

Look out the window.
Night sky.
Black sky.
Black mood.
Clear tears.

Rachel Cairns (13)
Sacred Heart Comprehensive School

POEM

I am lonely in here.
Disturbed with despair.
Darkened with death and illness.
Filled with dampness and trapped in a cage.
No one can see me now.
Distance long, and tiring track to cover.
Death can be lonely with depressing thoughts.
Only a vast emptiness in me.

Rabiea Rafi (13)
Sacred Heart Comprehensive School

ESCAPE

Illness and knowing you're going to *die*,
Brings *tears* to the happiest eyes.
Sadness creeps into your mind,
Torn between life and *death*.
Everything loses its colour,
Tiredness takes over your days,
And *death* becomes your only escape.

Lisa McCarthy (14)
Sacred Heart Comprehensive School

TRAPPED IN MY OWN DARKNESS

Black death
Cold heart
Empty room
Grey sky

Taken away
No escape
Black dress
With a stormy face

Hurting inside
But nothing shows
No tears
No blood

He's gone!

Elizabeth Nolan (14)
Sacred Heart Comprehensive School

LIFE

Life can bring depression,
It can tear us apart,
We feel trapped in our own dark, dull lives,
Our past memories can burden us,
Or maybe dreaded thoughts of the future,
Our ill thoughts cause misery and desperation,
We sometimes need a shoulder to cry on, to make us happy,
But maybe happiness is the cause of our pain,
Happiness hides away our true feelings,
It shields our fear,
Bottles up our worry,
Do we need *all* of this happiness?

Laura Jane Aitman (13)
Sacred Heart Comprehensive School

YOUR THOUGHTS

Sometimes you can get trapped in your thoughts.
You cannot get out, even if you are empty inside.
Alone in your mind, trapped in your mind.
A dark, dull scary cloud could form inside of you.

You may not have any thoughts but think they are there.
They may get you down, scare you, frighten you, but
They will still be there.

You will never get out of your thoughts but they
                              will never go away.
You might think if only I'd done this if only I'd done that,
If only . . .
If only . . .
If only . . .

Nicola Milburn (13)
Sacred Heart Comprehensive School

LOST IN A DREAM

You're sitting alone,
Drowning in your own misery and thoughts,
You can hear voices shouting things at you
Cheer up!
Snap out of it!
Shut up will you! You shout back at them.
Your conscience is telling you to do bad things.
The walls are closing in on you!
You're suddenly *trapped*,
You can't breathe any longer,
And then you wake up.
But somehow I feel lost,
Lost in a dream.

Kate Kilpatrick (13)
Sacred Heart Comprehensive School

No Escape

Trapped - darkness is falling,
You have to get out,
The black monster takes over my mind,
Death,
Death,
Death,
The thought of life makes me sick,
Emptiness slowly covers my life until there's nothing left,
Alone, I hear crying, it is me,
My pain is excruciating,
My world is black,
The trees are piles of ash,
The leaves are cinders,
Desperation,
Death,
No escape.

Victoria Houghton (13)
Sacred Heart Comprehensive School

Desperation

Silence, violence,
Tears and fears,
Have been building up,
Over this past year.
All the time it's a feeling of sorrow,
It makes my whole body,
Feel rotten and hollow.

Sometimes it's hatred,
Lots of fears too,
Missing and wanting,
Needing someone like you.

Deep down it's anger,
Closed up and trapped,
Wanting to shout and scream,
Get it all past.

Claire Smith (14)
Sacred Heart Comprehensive School

ME AND MY SHADOW

Wherever I travel
Wherever I may be
There's always someone, following me.

Whether I'm at the park
Or sailing the sea
There's always someone there with me.

If I'm kicking a ball
Or climbing a tree,
There's always someone imitating me.

If I'm in a situation
Where I need to be free
There's always someone who understands me.

Or if I'm in a dark passage
I may start to flee
But there's always someone who will run with me.

And when night creeps in
And the sun has gone
Me and my shadow are then as one.

Philip Hodgson (13)
Seaton Burn Community College

DEATH

Death to overtake her,
Death by night,
Death to deceive her,
Death by a fight.

Death by a gun,
Death by a knife,
Death by old age,
Death by life.

Death is upon us,
Death is near,
Death is coming,
Can't you hear?

It is approaching,
Quick, let's hide,
Don't go near it,
Or it will take you for a ride.

It's just round the corner,
You'd better run,
Quick, it's near you,
Oh no!
Its deed is done.

Sean Bates (12)
Seaton Burn Community College

FROM DESPAIR TO WHERE?

Culture, alienation, boredom and despair
It was always there.
Digging into him from all different angles.
It was all the truth.
Written down no one knew
Until it was too late.
Until he'd gone, gone from sight.
But not from mind.
Those words still ring true.
Always referred to,
Always remembered.
A constant reminder
Of the hell inside.
If it could have been read
One year earlier
Maybe he'd still be here.
February 1st 1995.
The day we all remember.
He walked out of that hotel,
Shattered worlds, broke hearts,
Left behind his truth,
Our truth.
Now all we've got is our memories
Of his truth. The truth we keep
That culture, alienation, boredom,
And despair.

Laura Hopcroft (15)
Walbottle High School

HOLIDAY

As I sat on the plane
Ready to fly
In a few minutes
I'd be in the lush, blue sky
I thought to myself
Tenerife here we come
Me, my dad, my cousin and Mum
I stepped off the plane
It was lovely and hot
I thought to myself
I'll like this a lot
The large, tall palm trees
Blowing in the warm breeze
When I saw the dark, Spanish men
I went weak at the knees
Holiday romancing
Nice dark tan
Lush Spanish food
And my cousin in his mood
It was the end of the week
And I wanted to stay
Even if it was only for one day
I said goodbye to all my friends
And I started to cry
Soon once again I'd be in the lush, blue sky.

Kellie Walker (15)
Walbottle High School

THE FOX

The fox head shoots
up from the ground
and hears the death
squeals of the hound.

The fox runs off
across the fields.

Its beating heart
begins to pound
as it runs further
and further away
from the hound.

Into the woods it
makes a dash
hurries out as quick
as a flash.

As its wide eyes
stare upon the ground
it watches the hounds
running round and round.

As the huntsman
blows his horn with
a stammer the hounds
retreat back to
the manor.

Kerry Hickman (15)
Walbottle High School

A SOLDIER'S BATTLE

Light broke upon the heavy morning dew,
The sun's compact, intense rays cut cleanly across my skin
Shedding my flesh of the cold of night.
Others felt this also, but most felt nothing,
As if their right to feel the sunrise had been taken along with their lives.
More light shone now, and the evening's spoils were now on show.
What had once been a fighting force, a strong force
Now coughed, spluttered, screamed out for guidance.

It was still only the morning, in fact the break of dawn.
Amidst the writhing and wounded, muttering and chatter were audible
But between those who could stand strong not a word nor a glance,
Those who were fit stared upon the atrocity of what had been done.
They knew there were tragedies yet to be uncovered
But nobody could have known what was to come.
The fate of the men present was much greater than their near past,
For it was the near future which would shock and injure them far worse.

To the sound of shell fire come the second wave of devastation.
Our side could not cope.
There were bodies strewn upon the battlefield as far
                                        as the eye could see,
Still, that did not stop the plight to save not ourselves
                                        but lives of others,
The actions of the men at that battle were united.
Out numbered ten fold, we all fought on.
Artillery cannoned further threats,
Merciless regiments dispatched and slaughtered our numbers.

Sunset arrived in a surprising fashion.
I and a few comrades remained alive, but not unharmed,
The enemy saw to it that almost nothing remained.
They had been obliging enough to allow me to see the sunset,
Possibly tomorrow's sunrise but I do not truly understand why.
Tomorrow can be my day for reflection, but today I could
curl up and die.

Jonathan May (14)
Walbottle High School

DIFFERENT WORLDS

I walked in the room, it was empty,
There was a silence from her laughter,
I stood and glared into the sky above,
I thought if I looked hard I would see her,
I heard my mother crying and crying,
My grandma comforted me,
It didn't seem to help,
A part of my heart was gone and wasn't coming back,
I didn't understand properly what happened,
But I felt heartache,
There were a lot of people coming in and out,
They were strangers to me,
I stayed at my grandma's for a few days,
This is when I realised my sister was gone,
She had gone somewhere where I wouldn't see her again,
I felt sadness and hurt,
I lost someone so special to me,
I had shivers going down me all the time,
Thinking about it made me feel sick,
Now I know she's gone forever,
Bye bye Becky.

Natalie Connell (15)
Walbottle High School

THE CAPTAIN OF ENGLAND

Alan Shearer is my hero
A knight in black and white
He's the greatest player in the world
His skills are out of sight.

Every time I see him play
He's always got the ball
His skills are just amazing
Especially in front of goal.

When Shearer scores
People shout his name
When Newcastle lose
Shearer gets the blame.

Everybody loves him
He's the hero in Geordie land
That's Alan Shearer
The captain of England.

Andrew Maddison (15)
Walbottle High School

A NEW DAY DAWNS

I get up early to go fishing
I walk down the harbour and look
over the sea. All is calm as the
ground is cold and wet with
morning dew but nothing will deter
the determined few.

Chris Dobson (15)
Walbottle High School

LIFE

Murder and devastation
torture, and sacrifice.
A black cloud has fallen
over the natural
world like smog over
a city.

Man has hunted for food,
now man hunts for sport.
He kills for a trophy
not for a meal.
His hunting now threatens
the extinction of many animals.

The wise young fox waits
with the early morning sun.
Not knowing that by sunset
he will have been chased
and tortured, his life stolen,
just so a man with a
stone heart can say
'Mmm, that was fun.'

Now only a handful of
protesters fight for their
rights. The world is in trouble
and no one can help.

Kevin Dodd (15)
Walbottle High School

EARLY MORNING MAGIC

I enjoy these cold October mornings,
The golden sunrise every day,
The quiet hour when nature yields,
Before mankind is awake.

The partridges rising from the dew-soaked corn,
The foxes running around in the dawn,
The rabbits running at the sound of my horn,
The cool, crisp air of this unsuspecting morn.

The swans asleep along the river bank,
The splash of trout after the occasional ant,
The leaping salmon up the wear
Freshly run for another year.

The geese are flying,
The stags are crying and,
The dogs need drying so as
The sky is turning red and
The mist is slowly rising,
I decide to return home sighing.

All this in a dawn that so few do see.

Andrew Ball (15)
Walbottle High School

WAITING

The look on the face
As time had now come
The fear in the eyes
Morning had begun

There was no way out
Not one chance
The sun had woke up
And it must be done.

Gemma Ions (15)
Walbottle High School

SCREAM

Her torment and anger thrown at the shore.
The sea, her loveliness no more.
Deadly pollution now her enemy,
Flocking birds their oil drenched bodies,
Stagger mindless and scared,
'No bathers' the sign, large letters bold in red,
Sea creatures now lying dead.
Modern life you are to blame
Since your pollution methods came,
You torturous beast, you rule, destroy
Barefoot children can find no joy.

Alone to fight her battle
Her screams and cries I hear,
Her waves, once pure and white
Now a black and dismal sight,
Scream, scream, scream, my beauty,
You have been robbed of your right,
Swirl and thunder, you deserve to fight.

Louise Quin (15)
Walbottle High School

SCHOOL

School soon came upon us
after the summer holidays
I woke up on Monday morning
with a funny feeling inside.

After I had my breakfast
I still felt ill
it might be that I was nervous
or it could be I was worried.

I got on the bus
I saw all my friends
my funny feeling went away
and I enjoyed my first day.

Hayley Harland (15)
Walbottle High School

AUTUMN

Colours turning, spinning around,
Spinning round till they touch the ground.
And when they hit it with a bop,
       They stop.

The wind comes howling, they go up again,
Spinning, flying, colliding with a friend.
But then the wind dies and with a big drop,
       They stop

Here comes the rain, making a stream,
To float on the water, they become a team.
But out comes the sun and with the last plop,
       The leaves stop.

Lisa Aspinall (15)
Walbottle High School

THE HUNT

Rabbits start to burrow, badgers run and hide
But the fox is running, running for its hide
It scampers across country
Past farms and towns alike
Running, running, running for its life.

In the distance the huntsman blows a horn
The hunt turns hard astern
It's heading straight for the fox
Not stopping nor likely to turn.

The fox runs on, no matter what
Its legs are starting to burn
It looks left, it looks right
But there is nowhere to turn or hide.

The dogs are nearly upon it now
The hunt nearing its end
With a deafening screech
One of the dogs manages to reach
And rip it end to end.

The fox just lies there now
Its life has drawn an end
It just lies there, its legs out spread
Its liver next to its head.

Robert Fenwick (15)
Walbottle High School

KATIE

She had the illness all her life, since she was born,
Couldn't speak, walk, eat or do anything for herself.
As the years went by, she didn't get any better,
She got worse.

It was when she was about seven and a half,
That she went into hospital and I never saw her again.
She died when she was eight, Mam and Dad's choice,
She was on a life support machine.

I thought life without her wasn't going to be the same,
I was only six at the time. But I missed her coming to
Pick me up from school with my mam, and at night,
As we shared a room.

I can deal with it better now and can understand it more,
We still send up presents at her birthday and Christmas time.
She is eighteen now, hardly seemed like a life at all.

I never did get to say goodbye.

Laura Robertson (15)
Walbottle High School

DOWN IN THE ALLEY

Down in the alley, the shadows creep,
What do you hear?
Children weep themselves to sleep,
What do they fear?

Down in the alley, the dustbins clatter,
What do you see?
Mothers and fathers ask what's the matter
Why do they flee?

Down in the alley, the animals cry,
What do they hide?
The black monster gave a long sigh
As it turned on its side.

Down in the alley, the noises turn soft,
What do you hear?
I can hear living things in the loft,
What do you fear?

Amy Smith (14)
Walbottle High School

UNTITLED

I heard your whimper,
And heard his shouts.
I feel your pain,
I feel his clouts.

Another day, another year,
Your master calls with a slipper to the ear.
I close both eyes to see your tear,
The tear of a raindrop.

A knock at the door,
And a quick hush-hush.
The blood of a paw,
As you lay there on the floor.

The stranger at the door had come too late.
As still as the night,
He carried you away.

Laurajane Gray (15)
Walbottle High School

LAS VEGAS BEAM

One in the morning,
but still it was light.

The yellow hum of light,
faded into the dark.

But one light was seen,
far, far above the hum.

Where the source was,
was a mystery to me.

Heading on for two,
our hotel was in sight,
and there, the source of that light.

Rebecca Nye (15)
Walbottle High School

NEGLECT

In an open field in the middle of nowhere,
I saw it standing there.
No warmth, no food, no care.
It looks so lonely, with no friends.
I think it has been hurt.
I can't really tell.
Someone needs to come and take it
away from this sad face of neglect.
I know it could be somewhere better,
not skinny, not sad.
Why does this horse cry?
Please don't let it die.

Katherine Aitchison (16)
Walbottle High School

CONVOY

Draw the blanket of ocean
Over the frozen face.
He lies, his eyes quarried by glittering fish.
Staring through the green, freezing sea - glass
At the Northern Lights.

He is now a child in the land of Christmas:
Watching, amazed, the white tumbling bears
And the diving seal.
The iron wind clangs round the ice-caps,
The five-pointed dog-star
Burns over the silent sea.

And the three ships
Come sailing in.

Robin Hall (15)
Walbottle High School

UNTITLED

My life a darkness known to none,
The bonds around me, my restricted movement,
I've seen it happen long before,
All the torture procedures to happen.
The adrenaline rush around me whole
The feeling of lifelessness has taken over.
My world black as death long ago,
As I see it will end in seconds.
A shimmer of death light above me,
The clouds that suffocate my breath,
My limbs now as cold as ice,
My living of life is now worthless.

Simone Banks (15)
Walbottle High School

THE DAY MY BROTHER WAS BORN

I remember, waiting and hoping for a girl,
but instead it was a boy,
I visited him at the hospital,
and took him his first toy.

He looked up at me with his big, blue eyes,
my mum said I could hold him for the first time,
I was only eight and he was so small,
I thought he would cry but he was fine.

Now he's no longer a baby,
he is seven years old.
But he'll always be my little baby,
even if he never does as he is told.

Lynsey McMeekin (15)
Walbottle High School

THE RABBIT AND THE HUNTER

The rabbit runs through the field,
using dense grass like a shield.
The hunter stalks, gun in hand,
his footsteps beating like a band.
The rabbit darts with all its might,
not giving up without a fight.
The hunter slowly raises his gun,
death does not spoil his fun.
The rabbit lies still and cold,
dead at only one year old.

James Bell (15)
Walbottle High School

SUNNY DAYS

The sunny sand and the long blue sea
Gently flowing just beside me
The many people running round
Gently playing on the sandy ground
The little kids building sandcastles
Their mothers sitting, having no hassle
Their fathers relaxing in the sun so bright
Carefully watching the beautiful sight
The soothing wind blows past my ear
So soon I know the end is near
The tide comes in -
We fade to blue
Now it's here there's nothing to do.

Steven Carver (15)
Walbottle High School

HUNTING

Here they come
guns in the air
ready to aim if their prey is near
there was a rustle, then a bang.

But no carcass was found
no blood was spilled
for this one day, they had missed
the prey had run, like the speed of a bullet.

'There'll be others,' the hunters said
'Yes, there'll be others,' they agreed.
God, help them now.

Laura Landless (15)
Walbottle High School